As chairman of the Frederick County 250th Anniversary Commission
and on behalf of the members of this commission
we are pleased to have a part in the publication of this book.
We thank the authors, Rebecca Ebert and Teresa Lazazzera,
for their efforts to have a permanent record made
of the history of this great county.
We also thank WINC and the Winchester Star
for helping make this book possible.
We thank you, the reader, for your investment
in both the history and the future of Frederick County.

From its inception as the northern gateway
to the beautiful Shenandoah Valley
to its present status as the Top of Virginia
this county and its inhabitants have contributed much
to Virginia, the United States, and the world.

We are proud to leave this legacy of our past
with the expectation that the future
will be just as exciting and meaningful.
The courage and hardiness of our
ancestors continues today.

We dedicate this book to all the citizens
of Frederick County—past, present, and future.

Donald E. Ratcliff

Tom Baldridge	Warren Hofstra	Sally Penfield
Pam Bell	Peter Krouse	John Riley
Stewart Bell, Jr.	Sam Lehman	Nancy Robertson
Michael Bryan	David Lewis	Margaret Rowe
Rebecca Ebert	Rhoda Maddox	J. Robert Russell
Michael Foreman	Cathy Monte	Bill Shendow
Amy Hammond	Frank Monte	Frank Taylor
Glynell Headley	Larry Mullin	Phil Walsh
Charlotte Hewitt	Steve Owens	Fred Zimmerman

The Winchester Star

Frederick County, Virginia

From the Frontier to the Future

A Pictorial History

By Rebecca A. Ebert
and Teresa Lazazzera

THE
DONNING COMPANY
PUBLISHERS
NORFOLK/VIRGINIA BEACH

Apple blossoms on Middle Road with Massanutten Mountain in the background. Photo by Rick Foster, courtesy of the Winchester Star

Aerial of Belle Grove Plantation on U.S. 11
south of Middletown. Photo by Rudy Rodgers of
Birds-Eye View

Copyright © 1988 by Rebecca A. Ebert and Teresa Lazazzera
Second Printing, 1994
All rights reserved, including the right to reproduce this work in any form whatsoever without permission in writing from the publisher, except for brief passages in connection with a review. For information, write:

The Donning Company/Publishers
184 Business Park Drive, Suite 106
Virginia Beach, Virginia 23462

Edited by Nancy O. Phillips
Richard A. Horwege, Senior Editor
Library of Congress Cataloging-in-Publication Data:

Ebert, Rebecca A.
     Frederick County, Virginia: from the frontier to the future/
by Rebecca A. Ebert and Teresa Lazazzera.
          p.   cm.
     Bibliography: p.
     Includes index.
     ISBN 0-89865-725-3
     1. Frederick County (Va.)—History—Pictorial works.
2. Frederick County (Va.)—Description and travel—Views.
I. Lazazzera, Teresa, 1957-   . II. Title.
F232.F75E24 1988
975.5′992′00222—dc19

88-20278
CIP

Printed in the United States of America

Contents

Stayman apples at D. K. Russell & Sons Orchards on Apple Pie Ridge.
Photo by J. Robert Russell

Aerial of Stephens City by Rudy Rodgers of Birds-Eye View

The old homestead of eighteenth-century English immigrant John Richards on State Route 604 in Mountain Falls, photographed in 1977. It later burned. Courtesy of Esther Cooper Moore

*Entrance to Sherando Park; courtesy of
Frederick County Parks and Recreation
Department*

Foreword

"What is past is prologue."

This often quoted saying sums up so perfectly the intent of the authors of this fascinating pictorial history of Frederick County on its 250th birthday.

The first settlement west of the Blue Ridge, our area rapidly became a crossroads of our young nation's dramatic growth. Momentous events flowed from one era to the next, from one generation to the next, leaving us a proud birthright.

As we celebrate the two-hundredth anniversary of the U.S. Constitution, it also is important to note that Frederick County was chartered a full fifty years earlier. Local representatives, nearly unanimous in their support for the Constitution, were influential in getting the state to ratify it on a close vote.

This is but one example of the impact local people have made on the important issues and events of our past. Over the years, Frederick County has been an amalgamation of many national origins, of black and white, and of many religions. As the county looks forward to the days ahead, may its future be every bit as rich and prosperous as its past.

J.K. Robinson

The Hon. J. Kenneth Robinson
Former Seventh District
   representative to Congress
Honorary chairman,
   the Frederick County
   250th Anniversary Commission

Above: R. Lee Taylor, curator of Glen Burnie and executive director of the Glass-Glen Burnie Foundation, dressed as Col. James Wood at the kickoff party for Frederick County's 250th anniversary on August 29, 1987. Photo by Teresa Lazazzera

Upper right: Glen Burnie on Amherst Street was the home of Col. James Wood, the founder of Winchester. Wood built the center of the house about 1750, and his youngest son, Robert, added the wings by 1790. In 1959, the house was restored and the wings were torn down and rebuilt with modifications. Photo by John G. Lewis

This page, bottom: Ducks at Green Spring Photo by Rick Foster; courtesy of the Winchester Star

Opposite page, bottom: Lake Holiday at The Summit in Cross Junction. Photo by Rick Foster; courtesy of the Winchester Star

Preface & Acknowledgments

This book is an overview of Frederick County's rich heritage from 1738 to 1988. It offers glimpses of the many people who shaped this community, its noteworthy events, daily life, and places of the past and present. We would like to thank the people who helped make this book possible:

The photographers who captured the people and moments of the county's past and residents who shared their photographs and recollections with us.

Dan Johnson and Irv Lavitz for the photographs and documents they copied; Rick Foster, Rudy Rodgers, Rich Cooley, and Alan Lehman for the photographs they took; the *Winchester Star, Northern Virginia Daily*, the Handley Library, and the Winchester-Frederick County Historical Society for the use of their photographs and archives; and John Westervelt for the cover photograph.

Members of the book's picture committee: Grace and Merle Moore, Katherine Watson, Ruth Rinker, Sherry Brumback Jenkins, and chairman Pearl Lake Ebert. More than five hundred photographs were located.

Joe Strohmeyer for editing this book; David Covington for his professional assistance and personal support; Warren Hofstra, Roger Delauter, Ben Ritter, Arthur Belt, Sam Lehman, Mildred Lee Grove, and James V. Hutton, Jr., for their historical expertise; Priscilla Lehman for the articles she looked up; and Edilia Lazazzera for her personal assistance.

Librarians, archivists, and museum curators who opened their collections and provided photographs and documents.

And a special thank you to the members of the Frederick County 250th Anniversary Commission.

We hope you enjoy this look at the county's past and continue preserving its history in the years to come.

Rebecca A. Ebert and Teresa Lazazzera

This page, top: Abram's Creek in eastern Frederick County. Photo by Rick Foster; courtesy of the Winchester Star

Aerial view of the entrance to Winchester at U.S. 50 (Millwood Avenue) and U.S. 522 in 1988, with Apple Blossom Drive to the left and Pleasant Valley Road in the background; photo by Rudy Rodgers of Birds-Eye View

The Loudoun Street Mall at Christmastime 1986. Photo by Rick Foster; courtesy of the Winchester Star

*Loudoun Street in 1930s. Courtesy of the
Winchester-Frederick County Historical Society*

*The same view as the opposite page circa 1952,
before U.S. 522 was straightened and the new
streets were built. Photo by Arthur Belt*

*Cupola of the old Frederick County Courthouse.
Photo by John G. Lewis*

CHAPTER

1

Now and Then

The Frontier!

Long before the Frederick County that we know today became a hub of towns and farms, rural communities and housing developments, shopping centers and highways, it was a sparsely populated outpost beyond the Blue Ridge Mountains.

Marketed today by local economic development groups as the Top of Virginia, it occupies 427 square miles at the northwesternmost corner of Virginia and measures thirty miles at its widest points from north to south and twenty-six miles at its breadth from east to west.

It originally included much of West Virginia and spanned northward to the Potomac River. Its northern boundary went from Cumberland, Maryland, to the Ohio River near Wheeling, West Virginia. Its southern boundary was at Augusta County, which was created at the same time.

To the west, Frederick County and Virginia went as far into the frontier as the British wanted or were able to claim. The General Assembly act that created the county in November 1738 simply said the county extended westward from the Blue Ridge. To some that meant to the Pacific Ocean; others said it stopped at the Allegheny Mountains or the Mississippi and Ohio rivers.

In 1745, more than four thousand people lived in old Frederick County. They were scattered throughout the present-day county and in what today are Clarke, Shenandoah, Warren, and Page counties in Virginia, and Berkeley, Grant, Hampshire, Hardy, Jefferson, Mineral, and Morgan counties in West Virginia.

Today, as Frederick County celebrates its 250th year, the combined population of the county and Winchester is estimated at 60,000 and is projected to reach between 74,800 and 88,103 by the year 2010. Both communities are absorbing, and preparing for, Northern Virginia workers who are moving west in search of affordable housing. They also are the destination of daily commuters from nearby West Virginia, Maryland, and Pennsylvania who travel to their jobs.

Frederick County of the 1730s was the destination of another migration—newly arrived English, Irish, Scotch, German, and Dutch immigrants who came south from Pennsylvania in search of good, cheap farmland. Eager to have the lands west of the Blue Ridge occupied to protect the colony of Virginia against Indian attack, Virginia Royal Gov. William Gooch permitted the Quaker, Lutheran, and Protestant immigrants to settle here and practice their faiths instead of requiring them to join the Episcopal Church, the state religion of England. Culturally rich, ethnically diverse communities were the result.

In the mid-1700s, Frederick County became the military and political training ground for George Washington, who came here at the age of sixteen to survey the lands of Thomas, the Sixth Lord Fairfax. Washington built Fort Loudoun during the French and Indian War and, at twenty-six, was elected to his first public office as the county's representative to the House of Burgesses.

During the Revolutionary War, Daniel Morgan's Riflemen from Frederick County were among the first who came to Washington's aid against the British. War prisoners were housed in Winchester and the neighboring countryside. In the Civil War, Winchester changed hands between Union and Confederate forces more than seventy times, and Frederick County was the scene of well-known battles, such as Kernstown and Cedar Creek.

In the years to come, Frederick County was the home of four Virginia governors and the birthplace of people who left to find their fame. Novelist Willa Cather won the Pulitzer Prize, Patsy Cline became one of the most popular female country vocalists of our time, and Adm. Richard E. Byrd charted the ends of the earth. Others went on to forge places of their own, such as Kansas Gov. James Denver, for whom Colorado's capital is named, and George Washington, a black man who founded Centralia, Washington.

Still others remained, making the county what it is today. In the 1800s, Frederick County was Virginia's leading wheat producer. In the twentieth century, it became one of the nation's leading apple growers. Over the years there were clockmakers and wagonmakers. There were ironworks, tanneries, sawmills, and woolen mills. Today the county's industries produce everything from light bulbs to the lids on soft drink cans.

In time, Winchester became a city and the home of the Shenandoah Apple Blossom Festival. The villages of Middletown and Stephens City grew into thriving towns. Hamlets, such as Gore, Gainesboro, Round Hill, Star Tannery, and Whitehall, became communities that maintained their identities despite a twentieth-century retreat from farming and rural trades and the closing of neighborhood schools.

From its beginnings in colonial days through the twentieth century, Frederick County has emerged from a frontier outpost to an agricultural community and a regional commercial center. As it prepares for the twenty-first century, here is a look back at its past and a look toward the future.

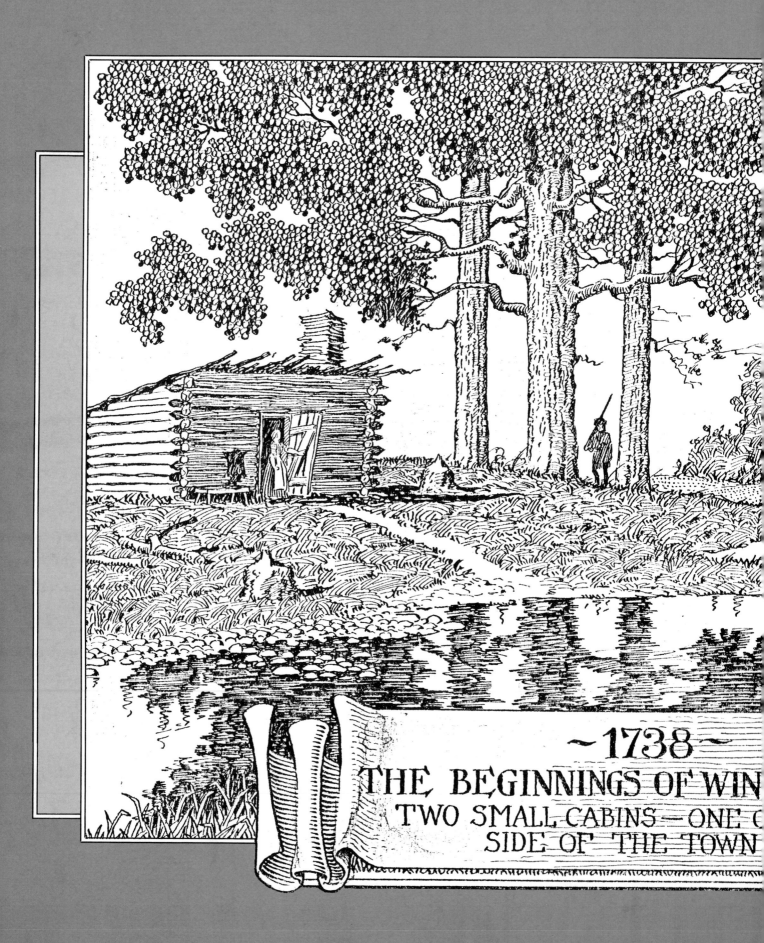

~1738~
THE BEGINNINGS OF WIN
TWO SMALL CABINS — ONE (
SIDE OF THE TOWN

Beyond the Blue Ridge

Winchester Evening Star *illustrator L. Neill Woods depicted the beginnings of Winchester in this 1935 drawing. In his early history of the Shenandoah Valley, Samuel Kercheval said an old woman whose last name was Sperry told him that when she first saw Winchester in 1738, it consisted of two small log cabins near Town Run. Courtesy of the Winchester-Frederick County Historical Society*

A highway marker at the boundary of Warren and Fauquier counties on Va. 55 shows where explorer John Lederer first saw the northern Shenandoah Valley and the land that later became old Frederick County. His travels over the Blue Ridge Mountains preceded the famed journey of Royal Gov. Alexander Spotswood by nearly half a century. Photo by Teresa Lazazzera

Frederick County is between the Blue Ridge and Allegheny mountains in the lower, or northern, Shenandoah Valley. Called the lower Shenandoah Valley by historians because of the northeast flow of the Shenandoah River, today most people refer to the area as the Northern Shenandoah Valley. The confusion arises because of the inclination to think of upward as northward, as on a map.

The North Fork of the Shenandoah River begins in Rockingham County and flows north on the west side of Massanutten Mountain. The South Fork of the river forms in Augusta County and flows north on the east side of the mountain. The two forks meet in Front Royal and the river converges with the Potomac River at Harpers Ferry, West Virginia. The modern-day boundaries of Virginia, West Virginia, and Maryland also meet there.

The Shenandoah River does not fall within the boundaries of modern-day Frederick County but flowed through the southern and eastern portions of the original county. Today, Winchester and portions of the county get their water from the river's North Fork.

The valley's waterways and rich limestone soil were significant to Frederick County's settlement. The first sixteen families that arrived with German immigrant Jost Hite in the spring of 1732 made their homesteads on limestone lands along the banks of Opequon, Hogue, and Cedar creeks and Crooked Run. Jeremiah Smith also staked out land along Back Creek in the 1730s and returned to live there two decades later.

Among those who arrived shortly after Hite and brought other families with them was Alexander Ross, an Irish Quaker from Pennsylvania who settled in Clearbrook. Hite, Ross, and others like them had land orders for thousands of acres from the Council of Virginia, which allowed them to act as agents in distributing land in the valley. The only stipulation was that they had to locate a certain number of settlers on the land within two years.

Royal Gov. William Gooch believed that populating western Virginia was a means of stengthening the colony against attacks by the French and Indians in the Ohio Valley. His promise of religious toleration cleared the way for German and Scotch-Irish immigrants and Pennsylvania Quakers, such as those who arrived with Hite and Ross, to settle the valley.

Alexander Spotswood, an earlier royal governor, also played an important role in bringing settlers to the valley. His heralded crossing of the Blue Ridge Mountains at Swift Run Gap in 1716 helped publicize the valley and encourage its settlement.

An earlier German explorer, John Lederer, made three trips to the valley in 1669-1670 and is considered its discoverer. In his own time, however, he was not credited with the discovery. The Englishmen who had accompanied Lederer on his second journey turned back, intimidated by the wilderness. They then saved face by claiming that Lederer had not found his lush valley.

Not even Lederer found what he was really looking for—like most early New World explorers, he sought a shortcut to the Far East and did not realize that a vast

These Indian relics were found in southwestern Frederick County about two hundred yards from Stephens Fort. The sharply pointed arrowheads in the center are four hundred to eight hundred years old and those with serrated edges are an estimated three thousand years old. Surrounding the arrowheads, clockwise from the upper right, are cutters and scrapers, bits for piercing leather, knives, and spearpoints. From the collection of Gene Dicks; photo by Teresa Lazazzera

Isaac Hollingsworth built Abram's Delight in 1754 and named it for his father, Abraham, who is considered Frederick County's first settler. Located off Pleasant Valley Road, the house is the oldest one in Winchester. Its limestone walls are two and a half feet thick. Abraham Hollingsworth, a Quaker, came to Virginia from Cecil County, Maryland, and built an earlier log house at the site. He is said to have declared the spot "a delight to behold" and bought the property from the Shawnee Indians in exchange for a cow, a calf, and a piece of red cloth. Winchester purchased the house and thirty-five acres in 1943. The house is now a museum. Photo by Rick Foster; courtesy of the Winchester Star

continent stood in his way.

When Lederer made his third trip beyond the Blue Ridge, he saw the northern part of the valley. He had crossed the Blue Ridge through Manassas Gap and, on August 26, 1670, set eyes on land that would become Frederick County in 1738 and break off as Warren County in 1836.

Indians were in the Shenandoah Valley long before it was explored by Lederer and other white men. Human history there dates back to 9500-9000 B.C. but few Indians ever settled in the valley. For most, it was a hunting ground, a battleground, and a north-south passage to other places. Among the Indians who passed through were Iroquois, Shawnee, Catawba, Delaware, Susquehannock, and Cherokee.

Abraham Hollingsworth, a Pennsylvania Quaker who is considered Frederick County's first settler, built a cabin in 1729, near a small Shawnee village on the east side of modern-day Winchester. The Shawnee, however, were gone by 1754 and returned to attack settlers during the French and Indian War.

Today only traces of the Indians remain in the valley. They left relics, such as arrowheads and burial mounds, and names, such as *Potomac, Allegheny,* and *Shenandoah,* which is said to be Iroquois for "Daughter of the Stars." Opequon Creek is said to be named for Opeckenough, the chief of a Tidewater tribe whose braves drove the Iroquois out of the valley and whose son, Shawnee, became the father of his own tribe west of the Blue Ridge.

In time, frontier Frederick County became an out-

17

This is a 1734 land patent from William Gooch, Virginia's royal governor, to Jost Hite for 280 acres west of the Shenandoah River above the mouth of Crooked Run. A German immigrant, Hite brought the first sixteen families to Frederick County in the spring of 1732 and had them settle along the banks of Opequon Creek. He acted as a land broker for the colony of Virginia and had the power to issue thousands of acres to county settlers. Courtesy of the Virginia State Library and Archives

post of colonial civilization. Responding to the petitions of new settlers, the Virginia House of Burgesses created Frederick and Augusta counties from the western portion of Orange County on November 11, 1738, and the act was signed by Royal Gov. William Gooch on December 21. Frederick County's court, however, was not organized for five more years. It met for the first time on November 11, 1743, at Glen Burnie, the estate of Col. James Wood, who founded Winchester and was the first court clerk. Twelve justices were appointed: Morgan Morgan, who is considered the first settler of West Virginia; Thomas Chester; Marquis Calmes; David Vance; Andrew Campbell; Thomas Rutherford; Lewis Neill; William McMacheon; Meredith Helms; George Hoge; Thomas Little; and John White. Rutherford, a Winchester merchant, was also named the first sheriff.

The court represented law and order. It enforced the colony's laws and petitioned the legislature for new ones; levied taxes, collected the money, and spent it; and rendered judgments in all civil suits and criminal cases. It approved the construction of roads and issued licenses for taverns (known as ordinaries) that offered food, liquor, and lodging. Taxes, licenses, and fines could be paid with money or tobacco, Virginia's cash crop.

Cedar Creek Presbyterian Church was organized in 1736, and the congregation met in a log meetinghouse built the same year. The house was replaced by a stone church built before the Revolutionary War. The existing church on State Route 622 was built after the Civil War and dedicated on July 28, 1876. Photo by Harold Gardenhour

Early settlers who came to old Frederick County with Jost Hite in 1732 are believed to have begun holding worship services soon after they arrived. Opequon Presbyterian Church at Kernstown, organized in 1736, is considered the first religious congregation in the Shenandoah Valley. The church there now was completed in 1897. It was preceded by three churches, beginning with a log church built on two acres donated by William Hoge, one of the earliest settlers who came with Jost Hite. The church that stood on the site before the current one was used as a hospital during the Second Battle of Kernstown in the Civil War. The church is on State Route 706, west of U.S. 11 south of Winchester. Photo by L.L. Ritter; courtesy of Harold Gardenhour

Irish Quaker Alexander Ross built this house at Waverly Farm on State Route 672 west of Clearbrook between 1735 and 1748. He and Morgan Bryan, an Irish Presbyterian, had asked the colony of Virginia in 1730 for rights to settle a hundred thousand acres in northern Frederick County and arrived with families from Chester, Pennsylvania, about 1734. Bryan took his family to live on Mill Creek, near Bunker Hill, West Virginia. His granddaughter Rebecca, who was born there, became the wife of Daniel Boone. George Fayette Washington, the great-nephew of George Washington, bought the farm in 1826 and is believed to have given it the name Waverly. The property remained in the Washington family until 1923. The house is now the home of Frederick County Board of Supervisors Chairman Kenneth Y. Stiles. He and his three younger brothers operate Waverly as a dairy farm. Photo by Teresa Lazazzera

Frederick and Augusta counties were formed
from the western sections of Orange County in
1738, and eventually twelve other counties were
carved out of Frederick. As the population in
the older counties grew, new counties were
formed and courts to administer justice were
established usually within a few years of the
county's formation. People who lived far from
the courthouse were vocal advocates for estab-
lishing a new county and a courthouse closer to
home. The counties that were created from
Frederick began with Hampshire County, West
Virginia, in 1753, and continued with Berkeley
County in West Virginia and Shenandoah
County in 1772, and Clarke and Warren counties in 1836. Parts of Hampshire and Berkeley
counties later became Hardy, Mineral, Jefferson,
and Morgan counties in West Virginia. Page
County was created from Shenandoah County
in 1831. Clarke County's separation from
Frederick County has been attributed to cultural
and political tension over a heavy tax for building a new courthouse in Winchester.

OLD FREDERICK COUNTY
IS NOW 12 COUNTIES

Map by Sam Lehman

Hopewell Meeting House was built in 1759 and is said to be the oldest building in the Shenandoah Valley to have continuous worship services. Alexander Ross donated land over the hill from his home for the Quaker meetinghouse. The Quakers are believed to have begun holding worship services soon after they arrived in 1734, and a log building that was destroyed by fire stood at the same site as the stone church on State Route 672. The building was enlarged in 1888-1889 but was once divided by a partition to separate Orthodox Quakers from those who had broken from original Quaker beliefs to follow Elias Hicks. Photo by Rick Foster; courtesy of the Winchester Star

Frederick County was named for Frederick, (upper right), the Prince of Wales, when the county was created from the northwestern portion of Orange County in 1738. Frederick was the oldest son of King George II but never became king because he died before his father. Augusta County, created at the same time from the southwestern part of Orange, was named for Frederick's wife, Augusta. Courtesy of the Handley Library Archives

Thomas, the Sixth Lord Fairfax and the proprietor of the Northern Neck of Virginia, once claimed a domain of more than five million acres that covered twenty-three counties in Virginia and West Virginia, including Frederick County. He got the Privy Council of England to appoint commissioners to determine the boundaries of his proprietary. He also hired young George Washington in 1748 to help survey his lands and opened a land office at Greenway Court, which is at White Post in modern-day Clarke County.

Fairfax was said to have preferred Stephensburg, now Stephens City, to Winchester as the site for the county seat because it was closer to Greenway Court. According to legend, he was outmaneuvered by Col. James Wood, the clerk of the county court and founder of Winchester, who served toddy to an unnamed justice with the deciding vote. The court chose Winchester and Fairfax was said to have been so angry that he never spoke to the justice again.

Fairfax never married. He remained a loyal British subject during the Revolution but did not interfere with the Revolutionaries' cause. He was born in 1693 and died in 1781. From the John Walter Wayland Collection; courtesy of the Winchester-Frederick County Historical Society

The Northern Neck of Virginia, which was inherited by Lord Fairfax, consisted of 5,200,000 acres.

PENNSYLVANIA

MARYLAND

Fort Cumberland

Potomac River

Martinsburg

Romney

Harpers Ferry

the Fairfax Stone

disputed area
Fairfax vs. Virginia

Hume's line 1743

Front Royal

Blue Ridge

Potomac River

Woodstock

Rappahannock

Alexandria

Privy Council line 1745

disputed area
Fairfax vs. Virginia

Conway

Rapidan

Potomac River

Rappahannock River

Chesapeake Bay

THE "FAIRFAX" LANDGRANT
8253 square miles

Lord Fairfax issued hundreds of land grants from his office at Greenway Court, such as this one in 1767 to Bryan Bruin for four hundred acres on Sleepy Creek in northwestern Frederick County. The county was part of Fairfax's Northern Neck of Virginia that Charles II of England granted to Fairfax's ancestors in 1649 and which Fairfax inherited. When Fairfax arrived in America in 1747, he found that the colony of Virginia had allowed the land to be settled. He quickly asserted his rights by requiring those who occupied his domain to pay quitrents and obtain licenses for their land. Those who wanted clear title to their property complied with Fairfax's demands, while others, such as Jost Hite, ended up in court. From the Lord Fairfax Collection; courtesy of the Handley Library Archives

This silver seal pressed into hot wax was the official stamp of the Frederick County Court for 146 years. The court justices ordered William Miller to procure a silver seal on March 8, 1758. They specified that it be about the size of an English half crown and be engraved with the arms of Virginia and the words "Frederick County." The seal was not retired until January 30, 1904, when the county court was abolished and replaced by a circuit court. Photo by Irv Lavitz

Gabriel Jones became Frederick County's first prosecutor when he was named king's attorney in 1744. He was not yet nineteen. Two years later he also became the king's attorney for Augusta County and held both positions for many years.

Jones was born in 1724 near Williamsburg and studied law in England. He lived and accumulated land in Frederick County before moving to Augusta County. A member of the vestry of Frederick Parish, he represented Augusta in the House of Burgesses. When George Washington ran as Frederick County's burgess in 1758, Jones took time from his own election to campaign for Washington, who was fighting in the French and Indian War.

Jones was elected Augusta's representative to the Continental Congress in 1779. He practiced law until his death in 1806. His son, Strother Jones, built Vaucluse, a mansion west of U.S. 11 and south of Stephens City, about 1780.

Historians believe Jones wore a bandage over his left eye because he either lost it or had a condition called "weeping eye." Courtesy of the Winchester-Frederick County Historical Society

Winchester, the oldest town west of the Blue Ridge, was chartered by the General Assembly in February 1752. It originally was called Frederick Town; Col. James Wood, the town's founder, renamed it for his birthplace—Winchester, England. On March 9, 1744, Wood laid out the town's first thirty lots, each containing half an acre. Four lots were reserved for a public square, which was bounded by the modern-day roadways of Loudoun, Boscawen, and Cameron streets and Rouss Avenue. Wood named the first streets, which ran from north to south, for British and American heroes of the French and Indian War, such as Braddock, Loudoun and Washington. Other early streets were named by Lord Fairfax for places in London, England. In 1752, Wood and Fairfax added fifty-four more lots; later they laid more. *Courtesy of the Handley Library Archives*

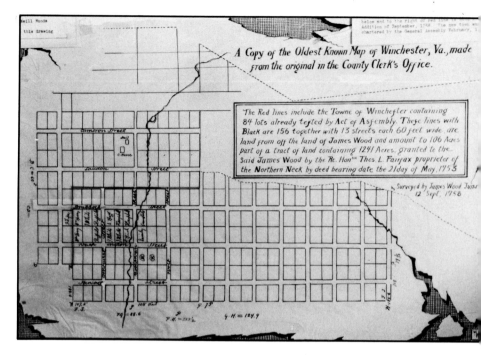

A Copy of the Oldest Known Map of Winchester, Va., made from the original in the County Clerk's Office.

The Red lines include the Towne of Winchester containing 84 lots already tested by Act of Assembly. These lines with Black are 156 together with 13 streets each 60 feet wide are land from off the land of James Wood and amount to 106 Acres part of a tract of land containing 1241 Acres, granted to the Said James Wood by the Rt. Hon.ble Thos. L. Fairfax proprietor of the Northern Neck by deed bearing date the 21 day of May, 1753

Surveyed by James Wood June 12 Sept, 1758

Colonial prisoners once peered through the airholes of this door at one of Fredrick County's eighteenth-century jails. The door was displayed for about thirty years at the old county courthouse after Trial Justice Alvin J. Tavenner bought it from a demolition contractor in 1938; it was again saved in 1974 when Kenneth Lloyd, a county employee, ignored an order to take it to the landfill.

The first jail was built in 1745 near the site of Rouss City Hall. It was replaced by other jails at the same site until the brick jail on South Cameron Street was built in 1845. Another early jailhouse door from Winchester is part of the eighteenth-century decor at the Evans Farm Inn near Tyson's Corner. *Photo by Wendy Gavin Gregg; courtesy of the Winchester Star*

Stephens Fort along Cedar Creek at Marlboro, where Middle Road and Cedar Creek Grade meet, was the site of Isaac Zane, Jr.'s eighteenth-century ironworks at the Shenandoah County line. The fort was built circa 1752 by Lewis Stephens, the founder of Stephens City. It was used to protect his family and neighboring settlers from Indian attack and was one of many small private forts along the frontier. The building's first floor is open to the roof, and there are two floors below. Men shot at Indians from behind the fort's thick limestone walls as women and children hid on the first floor below ground level. Water was brought through an underground pipe from nearby Marlboro Falls. T. L. Dicks and his son, Gene Dicks, once operated a museum at the fort with Indian, colonial, and Civil War artifacts. *Photo by Teresa Lazazzera*

Ye Public Lotts Winchester, Va. about 1757

DRAWN FROM DESCRIPTIONS GIVEN IN T. K. CARTMELL'S HISTORY OF FREDERICK COUNTY. CAMERON STREET AT THAT TIME CROSSED WHAT IS NOW THE CITY HALL PLAZA

KOONROD'S HILL

DUCKING STOOL

JAIL

COURT HOUSE

CAMERON ST.

COUNTY CLERK'S OFFICE

GRAVE YARD

BOSCAWEN ST.

THE FIRST EPISCOPAL CHURCH BUILT ABOUT 1752. REBUILT OF STONE IN THE YEAR 1762.

LOUDOUN STREET

Downtown Winchester is believed to have looked something like this only five years after it was chartered by the House of Burgesses in 1752. The log courthouse, forty feet by forty feet, was finished in 1751 and was the first courthouse beyond the Blue Ridge Mountains. It was at the site of the 1840 Frederick County Courthouse. Next to it and the Episcopal Church, a log chapel built in 1747 at Loudoun and Boscawen streets was the office of Col. James Wood. The jail was built in 1745 and stood behind the church. It was flanked by instruments of colonial justice: a whipping post, two sets of stocks, and a ducking stool to punish gossiping women. Cameron Street was farther west than it is today. Near the top of the drawing is Koonrod's Hill, which is now the site of the Frederick-Winchester Judicial Center. Koonrod was an early spelling of Conrad, the name of the family whose house once stood on the hill. Illustration by L. Neill Woods that appeared in the Winchester Evening Star; courtesy of the Winchester-Frederick County Historical Society

The troops of British Gen. Edward Braddock passed through Frederick County on their disastrous 250-mile march to Fort Duquesne during the French and Indian War. One of their stops was near Brucetown on May 5, 1755. They entered the county following what now is State Route 667 before turning west toward Hopewell Meeting House on what now is State Route 672. The intersection of those roads, facing west, is shown on the right.

After the British landed in Virginia in April 1755, they went to Frederick, Maryland, but turned back after learning that there was no road that led to Fort Cumberland. The troops instead made their way down the old Indian road that later became Valley Pike. After passing Brucetown, they continued west to Hopewell Meeting House, Babbs Run, Hunting Ridge, Gainesboro, Back Creek, and Whitacre, before going through Jefferson and Hampshire counties in West Virginia. The trip took a month. When they arrived at Fort Cumberland, Braddock used it as his base of operations. He lost his life and about one-third of his army when his forces were ambushed seven miles from Fort Duquesne, near the current site of Pittsburgh. Photo by Teresa Lazazzera

25

George Washington was forty years old when Charles W. Peale painted this portrait of him in 1772. It is the earliest portrait of him painted from life and shows him in the uniform of a Virginia militia colonel that he wore nearly twenty years before.

Washington was born in Westmoreland County in 1732 and was sixteen when he came to Frederick County as a surveyor for Lord Fairfax. When he left more than a decade later, he had become an experienced military leader and a representative to the House of Burgesses and was on the road to becoming the American commander of the Revolution and first president of the United States.

He was only twenty-one when Royal Gov. Robert Dinwiddie sent him to warn the French at Fort Le Boeuf on Lake Erie to stop encroaching on British territory. The French commander refused. During his trip, Washington learned that the French were building Fort Duquesne at Pittsburgh; his next assignment was to help build roads and forts to defend the frontier against Indian attack. Although Washington was made a lieutenant colonel in the Virginia Regiment, he was not given enough financial support from the House of Burgesses for the frontier defense projects and resigned after being forced to surrender to the French at Fort Necessity in 1754. He later accepted an offer to join Braddock's campaign and survived an ambush near Fort Duquesne in which Braddock was mortally wounded.

Impressed by Washington's military performance, Dinwiddie appointed him colonel of the Virginia Regiment and put him in charge of Virginia's forces along the frontier. The new commander returned to Winchester and made it his headquarters for the remainder of the war. From there he directed the construction of Fort Loudoun and a chain of frontier forts.

Washington was elected to his first public office in 1758 as Frederick County's representative to the House of Burgesses and was reelected in 1761. From the Washington/Custis/Lee Collection; courtesy of Washington and Lee University, Virginia

Long before he helped win the Revolutionary War and became the father of our country, George Washington was a defender of the frontier. This drawing, by Felix O. Darley, first appeared in Washington Irving's Life of Washington. A painting based on the drawing appeared for years on the ceiling of the Empire Theater, which used to be at the northwest corner of Cameron Street and Rouss Avenue in Winchester. The restored canvas now hangs in the lobby of the Farmers & Merchants National Bank on Cameron Street. A copy also hangs in the Handley Library. Courtesy of the Winchester-Frederick County Historical Society

Washington used this stone and log building at the northeastern corner of Braddock and Cork streets in Winchester as his military office from September 1755 to December 1756 while he waited for Fort Loudoun to be built. From there he supervised the fort's construction and other military operations during the French and Indian War. The building was constructed by Thomas Rutherford, Frederick County's first sheriff. It was sold in 1778 to Adam Kurtz and remained in his family until the city bought the building in 1908. Used as a hospital during the Civil War, the building is now a museum operated by the Winchester-Frederick County Historical Society. Photo by Teresa Lazazzera

Fort Loudoun was the site from which George Washington planned and directed the colonial military effort during the French and Indian War. It stood at North Loudoun and Peyton streets where the Fort Loudoun Apartments are today. At the time the fort was built, it was two hundred yards north of what then was a frontier village, but Winchester's limits quickly pushed past the fort. Fort Loudoun's location was mil-itarily strategic because it offered the last line of defense along the frontier if the French succeeded in capturing other forts deeper in the wilderness. It also was a staging area for troops from eastern Virginia and a depot for war supplies headed toward frontier forts. Winchester Evening Star illustrator L. Neill Woods did this painting in 1937. Courtesy of the Handley Library Archives

Col. James Wood, the founder of Winchester, was carried through the streets when George Washington was elected Frederick County's representative to the House of Burgesses on July 24, 1758. Washington was too busy fighting the French and Indian War to attend, and Wood acted as his proxy that day. This drawing is believed to have first appeared in Graham's Magazine in 1853. At the time of Washington's election, voting was limited to white males twenty-one and older who met land-owning requirements. Since secret ballots did not yet exist, a voter stepped forward when his name was called and announced his choice before everyone present. Free liquor often accompanied the election. From Winchester, Virginia and Its Beginnings, 1743-1814 by Katherine Glass Greene

3

Revolution

Freedom from British oppression had strong support in Frederick County. Nearly a year before the shots heard round the world were fired on April 19, 1775, in Lexington and Concord, Massachusetts, local patriots had taken a stand against British tyranny. When the British Parliament closed Boston Harbor in retaliation for the Boston Tea Party on December 16, 1773, Frederick County residents joined revolutionaries throughout the thirteen colonies with pledges to ban British imports and stop American exports to England.

Committees formed in many of the colonies were instrumental in mounting a united front aganist British encroachment. Virginians sent corn, wheat, and flour to Massachusetts and the Virginia House of Burgesses declared June 7, 1774, as a day of sympathy, prayer, and fasting. The next day, Frederick County residents appointed a committee to draft resolutions protesting the closing of Boston Harbor. The committee, made up of the Rev. Charles M. Thruston; Isaac Zane, Jr.; George Rootes; Angus McDonald; Alexander White; George Johnson; and Samuel Beall III, wrote the Frederick Resolves, an eight-point plan protesting taxation and obedience to laws that had been passed by Parliament without colonial representation. It predicted that the closing of Boston Harbor would lead to war. The committee also promised to stop buying British tea and most other products supplied by the East India Company and called on other colonies to do the same.

After war broke out, the Continental Congress called on the colonies to raise troops for the Continental Army and unanimously chose George Washington, Frederick County's former burgess and the builder of Fort Loudoun, as its commander in chief. He took charge in June 1775.

Congress also voted to raise ten companies of expert riflemen, including two from Virginia, and Frederick County was asked to provide one of them. Daniel Morgan was named captain of the county unit, known as Morgan's Riflemen. It was the first from the state to arrive to Washington's aid in Cambridge, Massachusetts. Congress had asked for sixty-eight recruits and Morgan mustered ninety-six sharpshooters. They carried Kentucky rifles, whose volleys traveled more than 250 yards, twice the distance of musketballs.

No Revolutionary War battles were fought in Frederick County, but the area was vital to the war effort. Its population swelled as hundreds of British and Hessian prisoners of war were housed at Fort Loudoun and in the surrounding countryside. Philadelphia Quakers who refused to take loyalty oaths in support of the Revolutionaries were banished and also imprisoned in Winchester.

A number of Frederick County residents who did not go off to war supported the Revolution on the homefront. Among them was Isaac Zane, Jr., who supplied the Continental Army with ammunition and stoves made at his ironworks at Marlboro. Money became scarce and Zane ended up footing the bill. His business still had not recovered from its debts when he died in 1794.

Zane was not the only one faced with money problems after the Revolution. Paper money issued during the war depreciated, giving birth to the phrase, "Not worth a Continental." Inflation and high taxes compounded the money problem.

Revolutionary War Gen. Daniel Morgan was one of the first to respond when the Continental Congress sounded the call to arms in 1775. He recruited ninety-six sharpshooters from Frederick County and headed one of two rifle companies from Virginia. They left on July 15. When they arrived at Cambridge, Massachusetts, on August 6, George Washington was said to have been so happy to see them that he wept.

Morgan was born in Hunterdon County, New Jersey, in either 1735 or 1736 and arrived in Frederick County in 1753. Standing more than six feet tall and weighing two hundred pounds, Morgan's large size and fiery temper made him a natural leader. During the French and Indian War he was shot and almost scalped; on another occasion he was sentenced to five hundred lashes for knocking an abusive British officer to the ground. When he and his men were captured at the Revolutionary War Battle of Quebec, Morgan refused to surrender and told the British to shoot him instead. He finally gave his sword to a Catholic priest.

Morgan and his backwoodsmen fought Indian-style from behind rocks and trees and found easy targets in the well-formed lines of British Redcoats. He distinguished himself in the Battle of Saratoga in 1777. At Cowpens, South Carolina, in 1781, Morgan made the best use of military tactics and inexperienced militiamen to capture one-third of the British forces in the South. There were several other Revolutionary victories in the South, but even Lord Cornwallis, who surrendered at Yorktown nine months later, acknowledged the importance of Cowpens.

After the Revolution, Morgan became a U.S. congressman, built a home called Saratoga in what is now Clarke County, and owned a mill with Nathaniel Burwell. In 1800, he bought Hawthorne, a house at 226 Amherst Street in Winchester, for his daughter, Betsy Heard, and lived with her until his death two years later. *Courtesy of the National Portrait Gallery, Smithsonian Institution*

One of ninety-six sharpshooters from Frederick County recruited by Daniel Morgan at the start of the Revolutionary War, Col. William Heth kept a diary that recorded the suffering of Morgan's men while they were prisoners in Quebec from January to August 1776. Heth also was clerk of the committee that drew up the Frederick Resolves. After the Revolution, he was a member of the Virignia Council and a delegate to the state convention that ratified the U.S. Constitution in 1788. He was appointed ports collector for Richmond, Petersburg, and Bermuda Hundred during Washington's first term as president. *Courtesy of the Winchester-Frederick County Historical Society*

Simon Lauck was only fifteen when he marched to Cambridge, Massachusetts, as one of Daniel Morgan's riflemen. He was one of six men who historian William Greenway Russell said was a member of the Dutch Mess, six Germans from Winchester who acted as Morgan's bodyguards. Lauck apparently did not follow Morgan to Quebec. He became a gunsmith and had his business at a site that today includes 303 to 311 South Loudoun Street. He also is said to have been an interpreter for Hessian prisoners housed in Winchester during the Revolution. Lauck, who died in 1815, was the younger brother of Peter Lauck, the founder of the Red Lion Tavern and another member of the Dutch Mess. Courtesy of the Winchester-Frederick County Historical Society

Frederick County nearly lost one of its most important Revolutionary heroes in 1951, when the town of Cowpens, South Carolina, the site of Daniel Morgan's famous 1781 victory, tried to claim the general's remains. The controversy received national attention and commanded a four-page photo spread in Life magazine. In this posed picture, Winchester and Cowpens officials depicted the dispute by lining up on either side of Morgan's grave at Mount Hebron Cemetery in Winchester. Holding a letter in his hand is Cowpens Mayor A. S. Moseley and next to him is Cowpens Attorney J. Manning Poliakoff. The Winchester officials from left to right are Cemetery President W. Nelson Page, Winchester-Frederick County Historical Society President Ben Belchic, Mayor Mifflin B. Clowe, Jr., and Cemetery Superintendent Oscar Harry. Photo courtesy of Mount Hebron Cemetery

An Indian fighter and Revolutionary War general, James Wood, Jr., became governor of Virginia in 1796 and served three terms. He was born at the Glen Burnie estate in 1741, son of Col. James Wood, the founder of Winchester and the first clerk of the Frederick County court.

Wood became his father's deputy clerk at the age of nineteen and represented the county in the House of Burgesses from 1766 to 1775. He successfully negotiated peace with the Indians in 1774. Wood and Isaac Zane, Jr., were the county's first representatives to the House of Delegates. Wood was captain of a county company sent to fight the Indians in 1774 and was colonel of the county militia at the start of the Revolution.

In 1777, Wood became colonel of the Twelfth Virginia Regiment of the Continental Army. He oversaw the imprisonment of British and Hessian soldiers captured at the Battle of Saratoga and in 1781 was put in charge of all prisoners in Virginia, Maryland, and Pennsylvania.

Wood was made a brigadier general in 1783 and was elected to the Virginia Council in 1784, where he served until 1796, when the General Assembly elected him governor. While he was governor, the Virginia Resolutions, a states' rights document written in reaction to the Alien and Sedition Acts, was passed. Wood died in 1813. Courtesy of the Virginia State Library and Archives.

Col. Angus McDonald came to the Shenandoah Valley from the Highlands of Scotland in 1746 at the age of eighteen and earned a reputation as an Indian fighter and a leading Frederick County resident. A veteran of the French and Indian War and Lord Dunmore's War Against the Indians, McDonald accumulated large amounts of land as payment for his military service. He was a member of the vestry of Frederick Parish and was Lord Fairfax's agent and attorney. He also was in charge of the Frederick County militia, led a county regiment that destroyed the Shawnee town of Wapatomica near Wheeling, West Virginia, in 1774, and directed construction of a fort there. McDonald later was made sheriff of Frederick County. A member of the committee that drew up the Frederick Resolves, he also founded the Masonic Order in Winchester. He built a house between Red Bud Run and Welltown Pike in 1762, naming it Glengarry after his family home near the Garry River in Scotland. When the house burned, it was replaced by another house with the same name. McDonald died in 1778. From Cornelia McDonald, A Diary with Reminiscences of the War and Refugee Life in the Shenandoah Valley, 1860-65.

A Revolutionary War chaplain and minister of Winchester's first Episcopal Church, the Rev. Alexander Balmaine performed the wedding ceremony of James and Dolly Madison in 1794 at Harewood, the Charles Town, West Virginia, home of Mrs. Madison's sister. Balmaine's wife, Lucy Taylor, was Madison's cousin. Balmaine was born in Scotland in 1740 and came to America as a tutor for the family of Richard Henry Lee, the grandfather of Robert E. Lee. After becoming an Anglican minister in Britain, he returned to Virginia in 1773 as rector of Augusta Parish. He soon joined the Continental Army as the chaplain for the brigade led by Peter Muhlenberg, a minister from Woodstock. In 1782, Balmaine became rector of Frederick Parish. He died in 1821. Courtesy of the Winchester-Frederick County Historical Society

Gen. John Smith supervised the many captured British and Hessian soldiers imprisoned in Winchester during the Revolutionary War and is believed to have used them to build Hackwood, his stone mansion on Red Bud Run, in 1777. He was born in Middlesex County, Virginia, and came to Frederick County in 1773, when Gov. Patrick Henry appointed him as the county justice. He was named county lieutenant in 1777, was made a lieutenant colonel in the militia in 1793, and became a brigadier general in 1801. In 1811, he was appointed major general of the Third Division of the Virginia State Troops, a position that he held until his death in 1836. He was Frederick County's representative to the House of Delegates from 1779 to 1783, a state senator from 1792 to 1795, and a member of the U.S. House of Representatives from 1801 to 1815. Courtesy of the Handley Library Archives

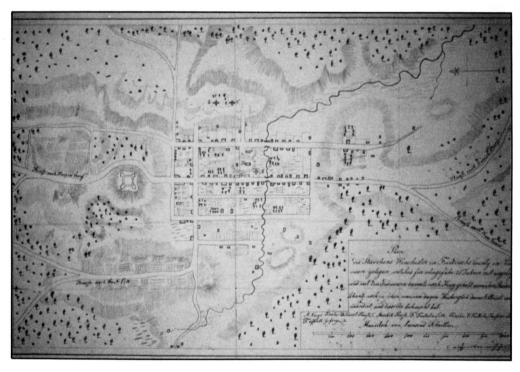

Andreas Wiederhold, a Hessian lieutenant captured at the Battle of Trenton, drew this map while he was a prisoner in Winchester from September 7 to December 9, 1777. The map shows Fort Loudoun, a markethouse, the jail, and the Episcopal, German Lutheran, and German Reform churches. Also shown are roads leading to Harpers Ferry, Parish Ferry, Fort Pitt, and New Town, which is now the site of Stephens City. Courtesy of the University of Pennsylvania

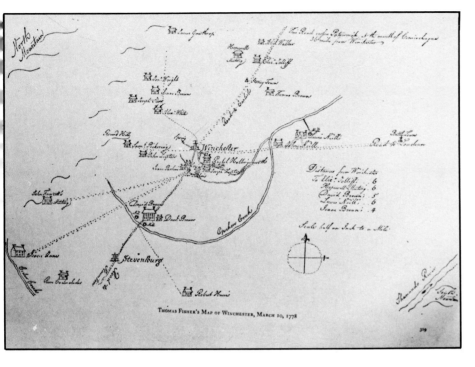

THOMAS FISHER'S MAP OF WINCHESTER, MARCH 10, 1778

Thomas Fisher drew this map while he and other Philadelphia Quakers, who were suspected Tories, were exiled to Winchester for about seven months of the Revolutionary War. The Quakers were banished after refusing to take oaths of loyalty to the new United States government because the swearing of such allegiances was against their religion. Among those forced to leave their homes was John Pemberton, whose brother-in-law, Isaac Zane, Jr., used his influence to keep the Quakers in Winchester rather than to send them to Staunton as originally planned. They arrived in Winchester on September 29, 1777, and were allowed to leave on April 15, 1778, after one of them died and the families of the surviving prisoners pressured Congress to let the rest go. While they were in Winchester, the Quakers were limited to travel within six miles of town. The map was drawn to scale and shows the sites of some local Quakers' homes and meetinghouses where prisoners apparently were permitted to go. Courtesy of the Pennsylvania Historical Society

This fireback from a colonial stove is one of many made by the forges at Isaac Zane, Jr.'s ironworks along Cedar Creek. The Marlboro business, which Zane purchased from Lewis Stephens in 1767, turned out enough kettles, skillets, strongboxes and ovens to supply the valley and export to England. During the Revolution, Zane went into debt supplying ammunition and stoves to the Continental Army and pans for the state's saltworks. From the E. E. Bayliss, Jr. Collection; courtesy of the Winchester-Frederick County Historical Society.

Five thousand Cords of
W O O D.

Marlbro' Iron Works, July 20, 1789.

THE Subscriber will give cash, bar iron, or castings, for cutting the above quantity of wood. Those wishing to undertake any part of said business, are desired to apply immediately.

Isaac Zane.

Four or five good Colliers, and a person who can make a compleat set of Pot Patterns, will find employment at the said works. I. Z.

A steady flow of wood and workers was required to operate Issac Zane, Jr.'s ironworks at Marlboro, as shown by this 1789 advertisement. Nearly 150 men were needed to cut wood, mine ore, and fire the forge and furnace. Thomas Jefferson, a friend of Zane's and a visitor to the ironworks, said the business produced 150 tons of bar iron and six hundred tons of pig iron a year. Courtesy of the Handley Library Archives

Taylor Furnace is the only remaining iron furnace in Frederick County. It was built in 1848 off what now is State Route 600 and across the road from St. John's Lutheran Church. In 1855 the furnace produced about five hundred tons of metal for utensils and tools. It also is said to have been used during the Civil War. The furnace is thirty-two feet high and eight feet wide at the base. Maj. James Bean, Sr., who built the furnace and operated an ironworks there, was the son of early Frederick County settler Mordecai Bean. The older Bean came to Frederick County in 1767 and began mining at the foot of Great North Mountain after obtaining mineral rights from Lord Fairfax. He formed a partnership with Isaac Zane, who built a furnace in 1769, near the spot where Taylor Furnace was later built. Bean obtained Paddy Mountain from Lord Fairfax in 1777, and eventually bought Zane's furnace. In 1816, Maj. James Bean, Sr., built the large brick house that is pictured in the right background. In 1931, Daisy Williams, a later resident of the house, wrote that the furnace was named for Zachary Taylor. Today the house is owned by Stephen M. Rosenberger and Jane Over Rosenberger, who is a descendant of Mordecai Bean. Photo by Rick Foster; courtesy of the Winchester Star

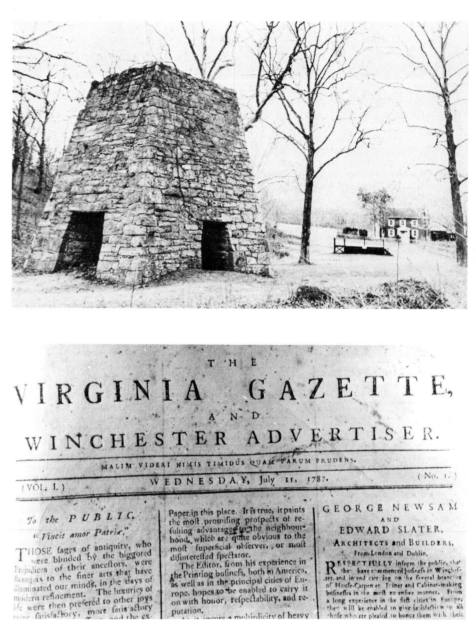

The Virginia Gazette and Winchester Advertiser, a weekly, was the first newspaper in the Shenandoah Valley and one of the earliest in Virginia. Its first issue was published on July 11, 1787, with its owner, Henry Wilcox & Company, promising to supply reliable news and the most current information on business and government. The newspaper got a new owner, Bartis & Company, in January 1788 and was later known as the Winchester Gazette. In the fall of 1788, the U.S. Constitution, yet to be adopted, was printed in full, with much comment in the weeks that followed. The Gazette was published until at least 1811 by John Heiskell. Winchester's first newspaper saw some early competition from the Virginia Centinel, which appeared on April 2, 1788, and was published by Richard Bowen & Company. Courtesy of the Handley Library Archives

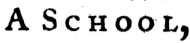

The Subfcriber having opened

A SCHOOL,

In Winchefter,
For the T U I T I O N of *Young Ladies,*

In every ufeful and ornamental branch of education, propofes to take BOARDERS, at SIXTEEN POUNDS per Annum, Virginia currency :—The fcarcity of cafh, and an earneft defire of being ufeful to her friends in the country, have induced her to make this offer. They will be taught READING, SPELLING, TAMBOUR EMBROIDERY, and all kinds of NEEDLE-WORK, at FOUR POUNDS per annum. WRITING, ARITHMETIC, GEOGRAPHY, MUSIC, DANCING, &c. &c. will be taught by the beft Mafters, to thofe who chufe to employ them. Deeply impreffed with the fincereft gratitude to the inhabitants of Winchefter, for the encouragement fhe has met with, every exertion will be made to merit the continuance of their favors.
Maria Smith.
Winchefter, October 21, 1788.

A SCHOOL

Will be opened in
WINCHESTER,

By the fubfcriber, on Monday the 3d of December, which he begs leave to recommend to the notice of all thofe who wifh to have their children furnifhed with a proper Englifh education.

IN this fchool the *Englifh* language will be taught grammatically, *Orthography, Reading* and *Writing,* with grace and propriety, and a complete courfe of the *Mathematics,* or any of the practical branches that may be required.

The ftricteft attention will be paid to the morals as well as the education of every pupil committed to the care of the public's very humble fervant.
FELIX KIRK.
November 2, 1787.

Winchefter Seminary.

WE the fubfcribers having had our Children for fome confiderable time paft at this *Seminary,* learning the *Latin* and *Greek* languages, under the tuition of *CHARLES O'NEIL,* A. M. beg leave to recommend him to thofe who may be unacquainted with him, as a perfon well qualified for fuch an undertaking. He received his education at the *Univerfities* of *Dublin* and *Glafgow,* and has DIPLOMAS from thence, as teftimonies of his abilities.

From the healthy fituation which *Winchefter* enjoys, and the moderate expence of boarding and lodging, we are flattered to fuppofe, that Gentlemen living in this, or the adjacent ftates, will find it their intereft to encourage an undertaking that promifes fuch general utility.

Edw. M'Guire, J. Gamul Dowdall,
Robert Wood, Frederick Conrad,
Samuel May, Ifaac Sittler,
Lewis Wolf, Tho. Edmondfon,
Henry Baker.

The public school system as we know it today did not exist until after the Civil War, but education in Winchester began in the eighteenth century with private schools, such as the ones advertised in the local newspaper. In The Schools of Winchester, Virginia, Garland R. Quarles said the first schoolhouse in Winchester may date back to 1748, when Col. James Wood recorded in his journal that he had purchased materials for a schoolhouse. It was probably for his own children and those of his friends. Courtesy of the Handley Library Archives

These stone walls in Mount Hebron Cemetery are all that remain of the German Lutheran Church, which was completed with funds raised from lotteries between 1785 and 1790. Two hundred years later, Virginia churches led the unsuccessful attempt to defeat the 1987 referendum for a state-operated lottery, but in colonial and post-Revolutionary America, state-sanctioned lotteries were an accepted means of financing church construction and new roads. In Winchester, Lutheran church elders cited lack of revenue after the Revolutionary War as the reason for the lotteries. The church built with lottery money burned in 1854. The congregation became Grace Evangelical Lutheran Church in the 1870s and now meets at 26 West Boscawen Street. Photo by Teresa Lazazzera

William Glascock, who kept a tavern at Stephens City, ran advertisements in English and German in 1789, hoping to attract customers. The Shenandoah Valley was a haven for Germans and other immigrant settlers in the 1700s. Courtesy of the Handley Library Archives

Early German immigrants who settled the Shenandoah Valley brought their language and traditions with them. Today, valuable family heirlooms, such as this family document, remain as testaments to their past. Its style is reminiscent of Fraktur writing, ornate black lettering that Germans used to document births, deaths, marriages, and baptisms. Large numbers of such documents have been found in the Shenandoah Valley and Pennsylvania, where many Germans settled in the 1700s. The writing often is accompanied by drawings of birds, flowers, or bees. Courtesy of Phil Whitney

Goldsmith Chandlee, a Pennsylvania Quaker, moved to Winchester in 1775 and made about forty grandfather clocks. More than a dozen have survived. Chandlee was descended from a long line of skilled clockmakers and jewelers. He set up shop in Stephens City after moving to the Shenandoah Valley from Chester County, Pennsylvania, and later opened his business in Winchester, at Cameron and Piccadilly streets. He crafted the mechanical parts for his clocks and designed their mahogany and walnut cases, which were built by local cabinetmakers. He also made sundials, such as the one pictured here, surveyor's instruments, compasses, brass scales, candlesticks, and tools. From the collection of Catherine P. Anderson; photos by Teresa Lazazzera

Frederick County was one of the places evangelized by Francis Asbury, the first American bishop of the Methodist Church and one of the founders of Methodism in the United States. Asbury, who helped to spread Methodism in the Shenandoah Valley, visited Frederick County on several occasions. He recorded in his diary on June 3, 1786, that he stopped at Milburn's Chapel, which once stood on State Route 662 near Stephenson and was burned during the Civil War. Asbury also preached at the first valley camp meeting in August 1806 at Indian Spring, the original home of settler Jacob Chrisman and the site of other early outdoor religious meetings. This portrait of Asbury was painted in 1794 by Charles Peale Polk of Annapolis, Maryland. Courtesy of the Baltimore Conference, United Methodist Historical Society, Lovely Lane Museum

Slaves were bought and sold in old Frederick County but there were fewer slaves and more free blacks in the Shenandoah Valley compared to the rest of the antebellum South. Valley settlers and immigrants generally had small farms and tended to rely on family members or seasonal help to gather their harvest. Large landowners in the eastern portion of Frederick County that later became Clarke County were more likely to require slave labor for their large crops. Unlike the farmers of western Frederick County, the settlers of the eastern county were primarily of English ancestry and had brought their slaves and the tradition of slavery with them when they moved to the valley from their Tidewater plantations in the 1780s. From the collection of Oren and Alice Snapp

October 2nd 1838,
Winchester

Received this day of John Bruce Esq,
Agent of American
Colonization Society, the sum of $300 for
Parent Society and the sum of $5.13/100 for
Va Colonization Society —

Thomas B. Balch
Agent of A. Colonization
Society —

The American Colonization Society, an early movement to eliminate slavery without offending Southern sensibilities, found some support in Frederick County as shown by this receipt of a donation in Winchester by John Bruce. The society, which was organized by a group of prominent white Virginians, challenged slavery without challenging property rights by raising money to buy the freedom of slaves and send them to Africa. But the movement was ineffective because the society could not raise the vast sums that were needed to buy the freedom of large numbers of slaves and met resistance from blacks who were against going to a land from which they were three or more generations removed. From Christ Episcopal Church Records; courtesy of the Handley Library Archives

This writing is intended to Testify, that Brutus has the liberty to call on me for his freedom at the end of any year he may chuse — in the mean time he is to serve me as usual, for the sum of 40$ per year, and I am to find him in every respect as I have always done —

Mary Meade.

Susan Meade.
Lucy Meade.
Frederick County — December 25th 1811.

Brutus, a Frederick County slave, was freed by his owner, Mary Meade, on Christmas Day 1811. Freeing slaves was illegal under Virginia law until 1782, when the General Assembly lifted a prohibition on manumission and allowed owners to free slaves by wills, deeds, and acts of the legislature. From 1785 to 1840, ninety-eight deeds of manumission were recorded in Frederick County, although some people ignored the law and freed their slaves outright. Others allowed slaves to buy their freedom. In time, whites began to fear slave uprisings and more laws were passed to restrict free blacks. Beginning in 1793, blacks who were not slaves had to pay a quarter for certificates of freedom. Courtesy of the Virginia State Library and Archives

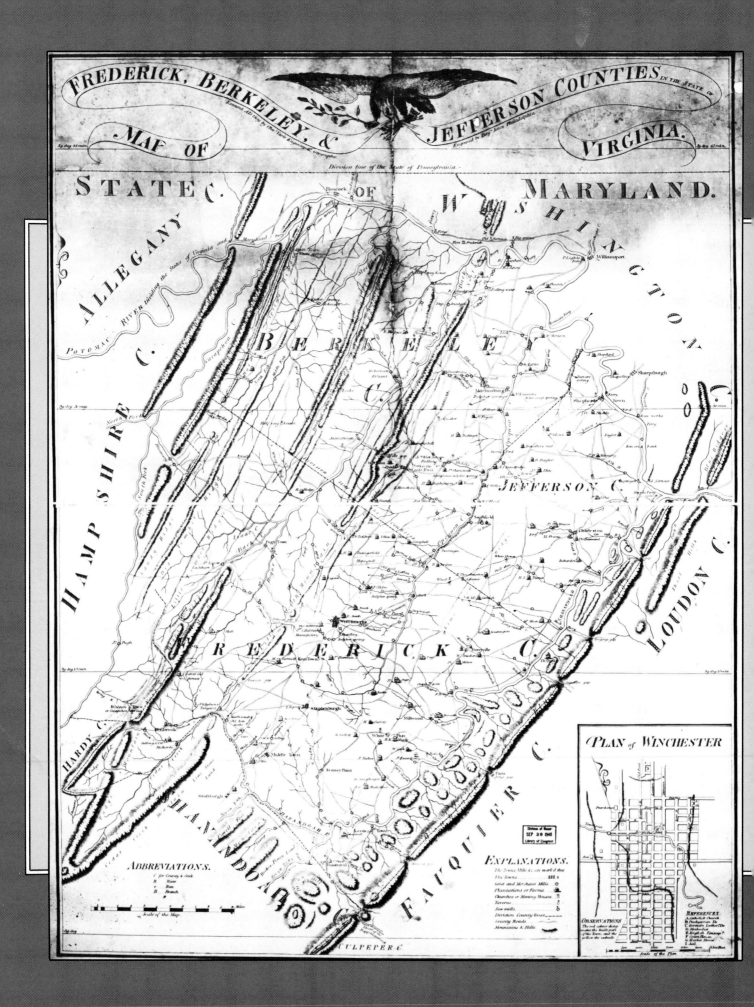

FREDERICK, BERKELEY, & JEFFERSON COUNTIES IN THE STATE OF VIRGINIA.

MAP OF

Division line of the State of Pennsylvania.

STATE OF MARYLAND.

ALLEGANY C.

POTOMAC RIVER Dividing the States of Virginia and Maryland

BERKELEY C.

WASHINGTON C.

HAMPSHIRE C.

JEFFERSON C.

FREDERICK C.

LOUDON C.

HARDY C.

SHANANDOAH

FAUQUIER C.

CULPEPER C.

ABBREVIATIONS.
C. for County & Creek
R. River
r. Run
B. Branch

Scale of the Map

EXPLANATIONS.
The Towns
Grist and Merchant Mills
Plantations or Farms
Churches or Meeting Houses.
Taverns
Saw mills
Division County lines
County Roads
Mountains & Hills

PLAN of WINCHESTER

OBSERVATIONS

REFERENCES.

Division of Maps
SEP 30 1940
Library of Congress

Long before there was a chamber of commerce,
engineer and geographer Charles Varle drew
this map of Winchester for an 1810 advertising
pamphlet designed to attract settlers and industry to Frederick County. It was printed by W.
Heishell of Winchester and aimed at Maryland
and Pennsylvania farmers who were seeking
better land. According to the pamphlet, Frederick County's population had grown by 3,038
between 1790 and 1800, for a total of 24,503
people, some of whom lived in what is now
Warren and Clarke counties. Varle also mentioned Zane's ironworks as a point of interest
and touted the county's fertile limestone soil,
especially in Winchester, Stephens City, and
Middletown and along Little North Mountain.
He said the area's principal crops were wheat,
rye, corn, and apples, and the main industries
were flour mills and distilleries. Courtesy of the
Library of Congress

Lack of hard currency during and after the Revolutionary War, coupled with a lack of confidence in the new national bank, led to the opening of state and local banks in the early 1800s. Many of them issued bank notes, such as this one-dollar note issued in Winchester by the Bank of the Valley in Virginia. These notes were promises for payment and not money. They functioned much as checks do today, and their actual value depended on the reputation of the bank that issued them and whether the bank had enough gold, silver, or federal money to back its notes. The Bank of the Valley in Virginia was chartered in 1817 and was the first locally owned and operated bank in Winchester. It closed during the Civil War and reopened briefly. The first banks in Winchester were branches of state banks—The Bank of Virginia, which was chartered in 1804, and the Farmers & Merchants Bank of Virginia, which was chartered in 1812. From the Mrs. Harrison Mann Collection; courtesy of the Winchester-Frederick County Historical Society

Winchester's nineteenth-century markethouse stood on Cameron Street at the present-day site of Rouss City Hall. It was built in 1821 and replaced an earlier markethouse. It was torn down in 1899 and replaced by City Hall, which was built in 1900. The streetlight in the center of the intersection was an early type of lighting developed by inventor Thomas Edison. The bulb had a carbon filament that required low wattage to operate and could produce light steadily for forty hours. Courtesy of the Winchester-Frederick County Historical Society

This old stone mill next to Abram's Delight now houses the Winchester-Frederick County Visitor Center. It was built in 1833 by David Hollingsworth, the great-grandson of Abraham Hollingsworth, Frederick County's first settler. Abraham, who died in 1748, operated one of the county's first gristmills at the same site and passed the business on to his son, Isaac. The mill was sold in 1870 to Ober & Sons, which operated a phosphate or fertilizer factory there. In 1884, it became a creamery operated by E. R. Thatcher and John V. Tavenner. Winchester bought the mill and neighboring spring in 1890. The mill became a pumping station and the spring was used as the city's main water supply until 1956, when Winchester began drawing water from the North Fork of the Shenandoah River. The spring was renamed Rouss Spring for philanthropist Charles Broadway Rouss, who donated thirty thousand dollars for the water project. Winchester renovated the building in 1987 for the visitor center. Photo by Rick Foster; courtesy of the Winchester Star

Transportation has been vital to the development of Frederick County. A crossroads for centuries, it grew in the years that followed the Revolution and especially after the War of 1812 and before the Civil War, when turnpikes, canals, and railroads were built.

The Great Indian Warpath from Alabama to the Great Lakes passed through the Shenandoah Valley. By 1750, the warpath's eastern branch had become the Great Wagon Road that connected the valley to Philadelphia. In the 1744 Treaty of Lancaster, the Indians gave up land in exchange for a road through the valley that became known as the Indian Road. Initially 175 miles long, it later was connected to the Wilderness Road that Daniel Boone built through Tennessee and Kentucky. Today U.S. 11 and Interstate 81 follow the same path as the Indian Road. The Valley Turnpike, which was chartered in 1838 and survived through the twentieth century, was taken over by the state in 1918 and became U.S. 11. Interstate 81, which runs parallel to it, was built in the 1960s.

Roadbuilding was revolutionized in the nineteenth century by macadam surfacing. Broken stone was tightly packed to form a thickness of seven to ten inches. It was first used in Virginia in 1824.

The Northwestern Turnpike (U.S. 50 west of Winchester) was chartered in 1831 and became a 273-mile road that linked Winchester to Parkersburg, West Virginia. It represented Virginia's desire to secure trade with growing settlements between the valley and the Ohio River. East of Winchester the road coincided with what now is U.S. 50 and connected to early turnpikes that went to Alexandria.

Other roads chartered during the same period were the Martinsburg Turnpike (U.S. 11 north of Winchester) in 1838; the North Frederick Turnpike (U.S. 522 north of Winchester) in 1851; and the Front Royal Turnpike (U.S. 522 south of Winchester) in 1848. The Berryville Turnpike (Va. 7) was chartered in 1831, but construction did not begin until 1848.

While the turnpike companies were building roads, railroad companies were also getting started. In 1826, the Virginia General Assembly passed an act that allowed the Baltimore & Ohio Railroad to build lines through the state. In 1831, the Winchester & Potomac Railroad became the second railroad chartered in Virginia.

45

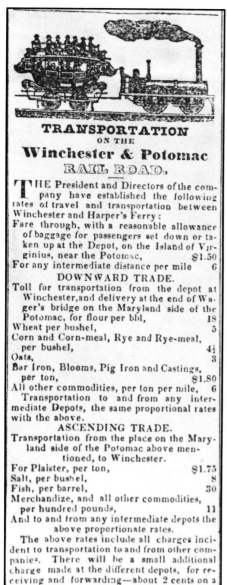

TRANSPORTATION
ON THE
Winchester & Potomac
RAIL ROAD.

THE President and Directors of the company have established the following rates of travel and transportation between Winchester and Harper's Ferry:

Fare through, with a reasonable allowance of baggage for passengers set down or taken up at the Depot, on the Island of Virginius, near the Potomac, $1.50

For any intermediate distance per mile 6

DOWNWARD TRADE.

Toll for transportation from the depot at Winchester, and delivery at the end of Wager's bridge on the Maryland side of the Potomac, for flour per bbl, 18

Wheat per bushel, 5

Corn and Corn-meal, Rye and Rye-meal, per bushel, 4½

Oats, 3

Bar Iron, Blooms, Pig Iron and Castings, per ton, $1.80

All other commodities, per ton per mile, 6

Transportation to and from any intermediate Depots, the same proportional rates with the above.

ASCENDING TRADE.

Transportation from the place on the Maryland side of the Potomac above mentioned, to Winchester.

For Plaister, per ton, $1.75

Salt, per bushel, 8

Fish, per barrel, 30

Merchandize, and all other commodities, per hundred pounds, 11

And to and from any intermediate depots the above proportionate rates.

The above rates include all charges incident to transportation to and from other companies. There will be a small additional charge made at the different depots, for receiving and forwarding—about 2 cents on a barrel of flour, and a smaller rate for other commodities. By order of the Board.

JOHN BRUCE, President.

Winchester, March 8, 1836.

This advertisement in the September 27, 1836, issue of the Winchester Virginian promoted the Winchester & Potomac Railroad's freight and passenger service between Winchester and Harpers Ferry, West Virginia. The W & P was the first railroad through Frederick County and the second railroad company chartered in Virginia. The company formed in 1831 and within five years had thirty-two miles of track. Farmers and merchants believed the W & P would be a boon to business. It offered the fastest means for transporting goods to eastern markets because it linked Winchester to the junction of the Baltimore & Ohio Railroad and the Chesapeake & Ohio Canal. While Winchester did become a regional commercial center, its importance declined after the B & O was extended west along the Potomac River to Wheeling, West Virginia. Teetering on the brink of bankruptcy and braving Civil War destruction, the W & P lasted seventy-one years before being sold to the B & O in 1902. On October 17, 1859, the railroad carried Winchester militia companies to help put down John Brown's raid of the federal arsenal at Harpers Ferry. Courtesy of the Handley Library Archives

Completion of a railroad line from Winchester to Harpers Ferry, West Virginia, and an 1836 announcement of a new wheat warehouse at Cameron and Boscawen streets went hand in hand. Heflebower, Roland & Williamson, which owned a wheat mill at Harpers Ferry, saw the railroad as a way to increase business because Frederick County's major crop was wheat. Apparently the company's plans fell through, because in 1846 the property, at the center of Winchester's nineteenth-century mercantile district, reverted to Robert Y. Conrad, who leased it to various commercial establishments over the next thirty years. Among them was Thomas Latham & Son, which ran a grocery and liquor business there during the Civil War. Capt. George W. Kurtz, a Civil War veteran who guarded abolitionist John Brown, bought the building in 1876 and operated a furniture store and funeral home. He added Victorian touches, such as the tower on the north wing in 1888. The rear wing was added in 1940. Winchester bought the building in 1968. From 1978 to 1987 it housed the offices of the Winchester-Frederick County Chamber of Commerce. Preservation of Historic Winchester mounted a successful effort to save the building in 1987 when the City Council considered tearing it down to build a plaza. Photo by Scott Mason; courtesy of the Winchester Star

Architect Robert Cary Long designed the old Frederick County Courthouse, which was built by 1840. The interior of the Greek Revival-style building is shown here. The Circuit Court met there until January 1963 and the General District Court met there until July 1984. Among the judges who sat on its bench were Henry St. George Tucker, who later became chief justice of the Virginia Supreme Court, and Richard Parker, who presided over the trial of John Brown in Charles Town, West Virginia.

The building was renovated in 1964 and today is used for public meetings. There are vivid accounts of it as a hospital during the Civil War. The courtyard, which then was fenced, was used at different times to hold Union and Confederate prisoners.

The 1840 building replaced the county's first courthouse, a log structure that was the first courthouse beyond the Blue Ridge Mountains. Built in 1751 at the same site as the existing courthouse, the original courthouse was the scene of a conference during the French and Indian War between representatives of the colony of Virginia and five Indian tribes; it was also the site of George Washington's first election to public office in 1758. Photo by M. H. Massie; courtesy of the Winchester Star

The Winchester-Frederick County Jail on South Cameron Street, built in 1845 to hold forty inmates, has been cited for overcrowding in recent years. In 1988, Winchester and Frederick and Clarke counties agreed to build a large regional jail on North Kent Street. The old jail was remodeled in 1907 and an addition was built about 1947. The jail replaced one near the current site of Rouss City Hall that was destroyed by fire in 1843. Photo by Rick Foster; courtesy of the Winchester Star

Before there were social programs to assist the poor and the elderly, there was the Poor House of Winchester and Frederick County on State Route 654, the Poor House Road, near Round Hill. Money for it was appropriated by local governments. The poorhouse was phased out as the social programs of the Depression began. It was built in 1821 for four thousand dollars, and the building was sold in 1947. Photo by Scott Mason; courtesy of the Winchester Star

Mount Hebron Cemetery is actually a complex of four burial grounds. The oldest tombstones, in the Reformed Church Cemetery, date back to 1769. Those in the German Lutheran Church Cemetery date to 1777. The third burial ground, Mount Hebron, was chartered in 1844 and initially covered five acres east of the older two cemeteries. Over the years it expanded to include fifty-six acres on a hill east of downtown Winchester and bounded by East Lane, Cork Street, Pleasant Valley Road, and Woodstock Lane. Among local notables buried in this cemetery are Charles B. Rouss; Judge John Handley; governors Frederick William M. Holliday and Harry F. Byrd, Sr.; Sidney S. Gore; and Judge Richard Parker.

The fourth cemetery, Stonewall, was dedicated in 1866 and is the burial ground of more than twenty-five hundred Confederate soldiers, including Gen. Turner Ashby. The four cemeteries and the ruins of the German Lutheran Church were enclosed by a black iron picket fence in 1891. Funds for the fence were donated by Charles Rouss, who also gave money for the limestone gate entrance, which was built in 1902. Courtesy of the Winchester Star

49

Known as the "Breadbasket of the Confederacy," the Shenandoah Valley was hotly contested by both sides during the Civil War. The South needed to control the 150-mile valley as a food supply for its soldiers and an invasion route to the north. The North wanted to take it over to cut off the South's lifeline and protect Washington, D.C., from invasion. The valley fell in 1864 when it was devastated by Gen. Philip Sheridan's Union forces. Drawing by A. R. Waud; courtesy of the Library of Congress

5

Civil War

Judge Richard Parker (1810-1893) of Winchester became famous in 1859 when Virginia Gov. Henry A. Wise asked him to preside at the trial of abolitionist John Brown. A graduate of the University of Virginia, he practiced in state courts most of his life. Parker was born in Richmond and later moved to Winchester, living on Washington Street. He was elected to the U.S. House of Representatives in 1849 but resigned to become a judge. He came from a long line of Virginia jurists, including his father, Richard E. Parker, a United States senator and Virginia Supreme Court justice. Courtesy of Clarke County, Virginia

Winchester and Frederick County are etched in the history of one of this country's most bitter struggles—the Civil War.

War rumblings were heard here as elsewhere in the nation, seething with hostility between North and South. Just as their fathers followed Daniel Morgan and George Washington, young men from the area were eager to march with Gen. Thomas J. "Stonewall" Jackson. Some served in the famous Stonewall Brigade.

Talk of war became a reality of horror and death with the First Battle of Manassas on July 21, 1861. The city and county became pivotal points for the opposing forces. At the entrance to the lush Shenandoah Valley, the "Breadbasket of the Confederacy," Winchester stood as a sentinel guarding the South's most critical resource.

The valley, with its macadam turnpike, provided a natural invasion route to the North for Southern forces. It was the back door to the industrial and agricultural might of the United States, as well as to its capital, Washington, D.C.

It is no surprise that both sides fought hard to control the valley. Winchester changed hands seventy-two times and Stephens City, then called Newtown, is said to have changed hands six times in one day. In all, six major battles were fought in Frederick County: the First Battle of Kernstown on March 23, 1862; the First Battle of Winchester on May 25, 1862; the Second Battle of Winchester on June 13, 1863; the Second Battle of Kernstown on July 24, 1864; the Third Battle of Winchester on September 19, 1864; and the Battle of Cedar Creek on October 19, 1864.

Most area residents were staunch Confederates but there also were many Northern sympathizers and neutral Quakers. Hostages were sometimes taken, women were banished, and buildings were burned in reprisal. Federal forces looted and destroyed many houses and burned the Winchester Medical School. Somehow, Winchester escaped shelling and survived the war with much of its antebellum charm intact.

Houses, churches, and public buildings, such as the Frederick County Courthouse, were used as hospitals for the thousands of soldiers who were wounded in battle. More than three thousand Confederate soldiers now rest in Stonewall Cemetery at Mount Hebron. Not far from them lay more than five thousand Union soldiers at National Cemetery in Winchester.

From the conflict emerged heroes. There were generals, such as Jackson, who was revered by his men and commanded the fearful respect of his enemies. There were everyday people, such as Tillie Russell, who saved the life of a wounded soldier by holding him all night on a battlefield.

The Civil War divided a nation and left much of the Shenandoah Valley in ruins. When the fighting finally stopped, the task of rebuilding began. Though more than a century has passed, a proud heritage on both sides of the conflict has been preserved by succeeding generations. They have remembered the Civil War through historical publications, battle reenactments, and annual ceremonies to honor the fallen soldiers.

A member of the Morgan Continental Guard, George W. Kurtz was one of the militiamen who stood guard over John Brown during his trial in Charles Town, West Virginia, and watched his hanging in 1859. Kurtz was born in Winchester in 1838 and enlisted in the Stonewall Brigade when the Civil War began. He became a courier for Stonewall Jackson, was promoted to sergeant after the First Battle of Manassas, became a captain in 1862, and was wounded at the Battle of Gettysburg. He rejoined the army after a three-month recovery, was captured at Bloody Angle during the battle of Spotsylvania Courthouse in 1864, and remained a prisoner at Fort Delaware until the end of the war. Kurtz established a successful furniture store and funeral business in 1868 and bought a building for it in 1876 at Cameron and Boscawen streets. A Democrat, he was a member of Winchester City Council for twenty-six years. He also was an original trustee for Stonewall Cemetery and at the time of his death was the oldest embalmer in Virginia. Courtesy of the Winchester-Frederick County Historical Society

Robert Young Conrad (1805-1874), on left, was elected to represent the area at the Virginia Secession Convention of 1861. He opposed secession and followed the wishes of his constituents by voting against it on April 17, when the state as a whole voted to leave the Union. During the Civil War, however, Conrad was an ardent supporter of the Southern cause and his five sons served in the Confederate Army. He was elected mayor of Winchester in 1864, but federal authorities did not allow him to serve. Courtesy of the Virginia Historical Society

John Bell Tilden Reed (1806-1895), on right, was Winchester's mayor during most of the Civil War. As master of the city's Masonic lodge, he presented Capt. William McKinley, a future president of the United States, with a Masonic degree on May 3, 1865. At the time, McKinley was an officer in Sheridan's army, which occupied the town. Reed was mayor from 1861 to 1864 and from 1873 to 1876. He is pictured here at the age of twenty-three. Courtesy of Robert Reed

Col. Wilford E. Cutshaw was an artillery officer who accompanied the Stonewall Jackson Brigade. He was involved in every battle fought by the brigade until he was wounded and captured in the First Battle of Winchester. Upon his release in a prisoner exchange in April 1863, Cutshaw was made acting commander of Virginia Military Institute. He was born in 1838 and died in 1907 in Richmond, where he worked after the war as a city engineer. Courtesy of the Winchester-Frederick County Historical Society

The grandson of Virginia statesman George Mason, James M. Mason came to Winchester in 1821 to practice law. He was born in 1798, represented the area in the Virginia House of Delegates from 1826-1831 and the U.S. House of Representatives from 1839-1861, and was later a U.S. senator. He was the author of the Fugitive Slave Law, a plank in the famous Compromise of 1850 that was designed to keep Southern states from leaving the Union.

Mason entered the Confederate Congress when Virginia left the Union and was appointed minister to England and France. While he was en route to his post aboard the British ship Trent in November 1861, U.S. forces captured the ship in Havana, Cuba. Bowing to pressure, the United States released the ship, which had been taken to Boston, and allowed Mason to assume his post. The incident is known as the Trent Affair. His home, Selma, on Amherst Street was destroyed by Federal forces and parts of it were used to build Fort Garibaldi, also known as Milroy's Fort. He died in 1871. From Public Life and Diplomatic Correspondence of James M. Mason

Cutshaw's Artillery, formed in 1974, performs Civil War reenactments and maintains the cannon in front of Rouss City Hall. The goal of the group is to preserve Southern heritage and accurately portray the original unit, which was organized in March 1862 and fought with the famous Stonewall Brigade. Courtesy of Ken Beauchamp

First Battle of Kernstown
March 23, 1862
Confederate Gen. Stonewall Jackson's attack on the forces of Union Gen. James Shields at Kernstown kept Union reinforcements from being sent to Gen. George B. McClellan on the Peninsula, southeast of Richmond. Jackson attacked, hoping to reoccupy Winchester and regain control of the valley. But he was misinformed about the number of Union troops and found his three thousand Confederates outnumbered two-to-one by Shields' Union soldiers. It is considered to be Jackson's only military defeat.

Jackson's defeat by Shields delighted the Union so much that President Abraham Lincoln sent Secretary of State William H. Seward, pictured above, and Secretary of War Edwin M. Stanton to Winchester to congratulate the victors. Upon his return to Washington, Seward was asked what he felt about Winchester and said, "The men are all in the army and the women are the devil!" Diaries show that local women demonstrated their support for the Southern cause whenever possible, to the irritation of Union authorities. From The Portrait Gallery of the War

A diary kept by Cornelia Peake McDonald (1822-1909) documented the Union occupation of Winchester from March 1862 to June 1863. She added her reminiscences to the diary in 1875, and her son, Hunter, published it in 1934. It offers vivid accounts of how local residents dealt with armies on both sides and graphic glimpses of wartime horrors.

McDonald lived at Hawthorne on Amherst Street. Her husband joined the Confederate Army, leaving her to manage the household and care for their seven small children. This is how she described Winchester after the First Battle of Kernstown: "Every available place was turned into a hospital, the courthouse was full, the vacant banks, and even the churches." She also told what she found at the courthouse: a porch strewn with dead soldiers; the horribly mutilated bodies of the wounded inside and the sound of men whose limbs were being amputated; and her dress brushing against amputated limbs heaped by a door.

McDonald fled to Lexington with her family in 1863 and never returned to Winchester. From Cornelia McDonald, A Diary With Reminiscences of the War and Refugee Life in the Shenandoah Valley 1860-1865

Angus William McDonald, the husband of Cornelia McDonald, was sixty-two years old when the Civil War began. In June 1861, he organized the Seventh Regiment of Virginia Cavalry, which became known as the Laurel Brigade. He was its colonel until later that year, when severe rheumatism forced him to resign. McDonald was then assigned to the Confederate War Department in Richmond. He joined his wife, who had fled from Winchester, in Lexington in December 1863. He was captured by Union Gen. David Hunter in 1864 and died later that year. From Cornelia McDonald, A Diary With Reminiscences of the War and Refugee Life in the Shenandoah Valley 1860-1865

The First Battle of Winchester
May 25, 1862
Following his victory over Union troops in Front Royal, Stonewall Jackson attacked the Union forces of Gen. Nathaniel P. Banks south of Winchester on May 25. The battle was a significant win in Jackson's Valley Campaign, which established him as one of the best field commanders of the Civil War. Fighting erupted when Banks's men, who were retreating from Strasburg to Martinsburg and Harpers Ferry, West Virginia, were hit by Confederate forces. Jackson chased the Union troops to Harpers Ferry before withdrawing in the face of heavy reinforcements.

A button was missing from the coat of Gen. Thomas J. "Stonewall" Jackson when he posed for this photograph in 1862. The general sewed it back on slightly askew and had his picture taken by photographer Nathaniel Routzahn. This was Mary Anna Morrison Jackson's favorite photo of her husband. From the Charles Affleck Collection; courtesy of the Winchester-Frederick County Historical Society

Confederate Gen. Stonewall Jackson was given this house on North Braddock Street in Winchester to use as his headquarters from November 1861 to the spring of 1862, when he left for his famous Valley Campaign. The house was built in 1854 and was owned by Col. Lewis Tilghman Moore. It is now a museum operated by the Winchester-Frederick County Historical Society. Photo by Scott Mason; courtesy of the Winchester Star.

"Jackson at Winchester" was painted by William Washington in the 1870s. It depicts the Confederate general being hailed by local residents at the time of the First Battle of Winchester. Courtesy of the Valentine Museum, Richmond

Winchester doctor Hunter Holmes McGuire (1835-1900) was Stonewall Jackson's personal physician and medical director of the Army of the Shenandoah. When Jackson was accidentally shot by his own men at Chancellorsville in 1863, McGuire treated him and was with him when he died.

When frictions developed between Northern and Southern students at the Jefferson Medical School in Philadelphia over the hanging of John Brown, McGuire led three hundred Southern students to the Medical College of Virginia in Richmond. During the war, he coordinated a medical service that used captured supplies and organized temporary field hospitals at battle sites. He also established a policy that viewed medical officers as noncombatants and allowed for their exchange so wounded soldiers could receive medical care. After Jackson's death, McGuire became medical director of the Army of Northern Virginia.

McGuire moved to Richmond after the war, where he established St. Luke's Home for the Sick, one of the first private hospitals in the South. He was president of the American Medical Association. He was born in 1835 and died in 1900. Courtesy of the Handley Library Archives

President Lincoln appointed Nathaniel P. Banks major general in 1861. While commander of Union forces in Winchester, Banks ordered the destruction of the Winchester Medical College at Stewart and Boscawen streets. He learned that students had used the body of John Brown's son as a dissecting cadaver and burned the school in retaliation. Banks, speaker of the U.S. House of Representatives before the war, lost 30 percent of his forces when he faced Gen. Stonewall Jackson's troops in the Shenandoah Valley and became known as "Jackson's commissary" because of the many Union supply wagons that the Confederates confiscated. From Portrait Gallery of the War

Star Fort
Built in 1861 as an emplacement for weapons by Gen. Stonewall Jackson's Confederate troops, Star Fort on U.S. 522 north of Winchester was originally called Fort Alabama for the first Southern troops to arrive in Winchester from outside Virginia. Union Gen. Robert H. Milroy extended the emplacement, which was used to house troops and ordnance. The name comes from the unique shape of the fort, which is now being restored by Middlesex Artillery, Fleets Battery and the Living Historians for Virginia. From the Virginia and William Miller Collection; courtesy of the Winchester-Frederick County Historical Society

Second Battle of Winchester
June 14-15, 1863
Before Gen. Robert E. Lee, commander of the Army of Northern Virginia, launched his ill-fated invasion of Gettysburg, Pennsylvania, he ordered the Army of Northern Virginia's Second Corps to clear the Shenandoah Valley of Union troops.

Gen. Richard S. Ewell complied by attacking Gen. Robert H. Milroy's army on June 14. The Union forces fled that night and were defeated early the next morning near Stephenson's Depot.

An Indiana lawyer until the war began, Robert H. Milroy raised the Ninth Indiana Volunteer Regiment and became its colonel in 1861. His harsh rule of Winchester from January 1 to June 14, 1863, made him one of the most disliked Union commanders in the area. His control ended with the Second Battle of Winchester. While retreating from Confederate Gen. Richard Ewell at Stephenson's Depot, Milroy lost thirty-four hundred Confederate prisoners, twenty-three pieces of artillery and many of his troops. Milroy escaped to Harpers Ferry, West Virginia, with members of his cavalry, but he never again was a field commander. Courtesy of the Virginia State Library

Third Battle of Winchester
September 19, 1864
At dawn on September 19, 1864, the Union forces commanded by Gen. Philip Sheridan attacked Confederate troops led by Gen. Jubal A. Early.

Outnumbered Confederates withstood the Union attacks north and east of Winchester until a cavalry charge broke the Confederate lines in the late afternoon. Early was driven south and the Union Army took control of the city.

Quaker schoolteacher Rebecca L. Wright was known for her Union sympathies. A black spy asked the young Winchester woman to be an informant for Union Gen. Philip Sheridan in September 1864, and she soon passed on information she got from a Confederate soldier. Based on Wright's information, Sheridan realized that the forces of Confederate Gen. Jubal A. Early were not as large as he had thought and decided to cross Opequon Creek at the Millbank House to attack Early at Winchester on September 19, 1864.

Sheridan thanked Wright afterward in person and gave her a gold watch as a memento. With Sheridan's help, she also got a job in the U.S. Treasury Department after the war and lived in Washington for the rest of her life. Courtesy of the Handley Library Archives

Hackwood, the stone mansion that Gen. John Smith built during the Revolutionary War, was at the center of Civil War fighting during the Third Battle of Winchester on September 19, 1864. This is how the house looked after the battle. It has since been restored. Photo by James B. Wortham of Winchester, courtesy of the Massachusetts Military Order of the Loyal Legion of the United States, U.S. Army Military History Institute, Carlisle Barracks, Pennsylvania

Second Battle of Kernstown
July 24, 1864
When Confederate Gen. Jubal A. Early returned from Washington, D.C., the Union troops that had pursued him made camp at Kernstown. Several days later, on July 24, 1864, Early attacked the Union forces under the command of Gen. George Crook, driving them north to Martinsburg, West Virginia, and giving Confederate troops control of the Northern Shenandoah Valley until the Third Battle of Winchester.

Gen. Jubal A. Early, known as "Old Jube," played an important role in the Confederacy's attempt to rid the Shenandoah Valley of Union forces in 1864. As division commander of the Second Corps of the Army of Northern Virginia in the summer of 1864, Early harassed Union troops in Martinsburg, West Virginia, and in the fall led the Confederate Army in the Second Battle of Winchester and in battles at Fisher's Hill and Cedar Creek. He fled to Mexico when the South surrendered, but he later returned to Lynchburg, where he died in 1894. He boasted that he never surrendered and would never be "reconstructed." Courtesy of the Virginia State Library

Battle of Cedar Creek
October 19, 1864
Just before dawn on October 19, 1864, the army of Confederate Gen. Jubal A. Early attacked the Union troops of Gen. Philip Sheridan in their camps north of Cedar Creek.

The Union forces were routed and driven north of Middletown, where they regrouped. In the late afternoon, a Union counterattack drove the Southern troops south of Strasburg. As a result, Union troops controlled the valley until the end of the war.

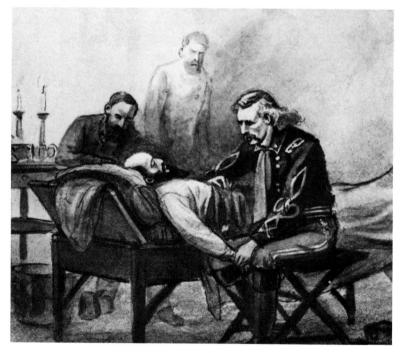

A feisty fighter, Union Gen. Philip Henry Sheridan was given almost fifty thousand troops in 1864 to destroy the Shenandoah Valley. Gen. Ulysses S. Grant told him to make it so desolate a "crow will have to carry his own provisions when flying over it" and "to close the back door on Washington forever."

Sheridan successfully routed Early and his Confederates and sent them "whirling southward through Winchester" at the Third Battle of Winchester on September 19, 1864. His final victory over Early was at Cedar Creek, when he rode from Winchester to rally his retreating soldiers and turned an apparent defeat into a victory.

Sheridan's military rule of Winchester was strict and sometimes cruel. His rise in the army continued after the war. In 1884, he became the commanding general of the U.S. Army. Courtesy of the Library of Congress

Stephen Dodson Ramseur, a young Confederate general from North Carolina, was wounded at the Battle of Cedar Creek. Union soldiers took him to die at Belle Grove, a mansion south of Middletown that Gen. Philip Sheridan used as his headquarters after the battle. As Ramseur lay dying, Union officer George A. Custer, an old friend from West Point and later a legendary Indian fighter, sat with him.

Ramseur's body was returned to the Confederates and his death was greatly mourned by the South. He was the youngest West Point graduate to be a major general in the Confederate Army. He also played an important part in every battle in or near Winchester. At the Battle of Cedar Creek, his men routed Gen. George Crook's Eighth U.S. Army Corps. The Confederates, however, stopped to collect badly needed supplies and the Union forces were able to regroup and mount a successful counterattack. Courtesy of the Western Reserve Historical Society

Civil War soldiers of the Sixth U.S. Army Corps held a reunion at Belle Grove in 1885. The house was at the center of the Battle of Cedar Creek. It was used as a hospital and Confederate General Stephen D. Ramseur died there.

Now owned by the National Trust for Historic Preservation, Belle Grove has operated as a museum since 1967. It is on U.S. 11 south of Middletown. The house was built in 1794 by Isaac Hite, Jr., the grandson of pioneer Jost Hite. James and Dolly Madison spent part of their honeymoon on the estate just before Belle Grove was built and stayed at an older house that is no longer standing. Isaac Hite, Jr., was married to Madison's sister, Eleanor. Photo by James B. Worthham of Winchester; courtesy of the Massachusetts Military Order of the Loyal Legion of the United States, U.S. Army Military History Institute, Carlisle Barracks, Pennsylvania

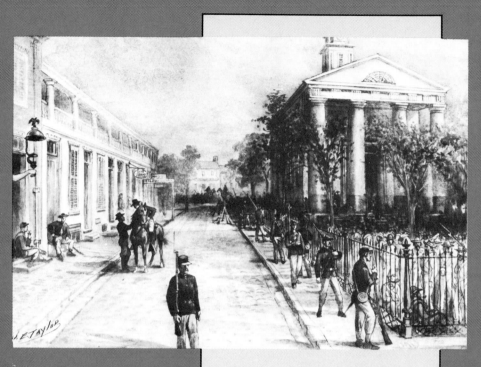

These Confederate prisoners were captured at the Third Battle of Winchester. They were held in the front yard of the old Frederick County Courthouse before being taken to Northern prisons. During the war, both sides used the yard as a holding facility and the courthouse was used as a hospital. Courtesy of the Western Reserve Historical Society

The Union Army used the Taylor Hotel in downtown Winchester as a military headquarters and hospital during the Civil War. This photograph was taken in April 1862, when Leonard's Brigade was quartered there. McCrory's variety store moved to the site in 1924 and is still there. The hotel was operated by Bushrod Taylor. He bought the McGuire Hotel, an earlier hotel at the same site, in 1830. He operated it until the building was destroyed by a fire in 1845 and replaced it with the Taylor Hotel. Courtesy of the Massachusetts Military Order of the Loyal Legion of the United States, U.S. Army Military History Institute, Carlisle Barracks, Pennsylvania

At the end of the war, local women sought a proper resting place for fallen Confederate soldiers, whose bodies were buried in fields and other cemeteries throughout the area. In May 1865, Mary Dunbar Williams and Eleanor Williams Boyd established the Ladies Confederate Memorial Association, which developed Stonewall Cemetery.

The cemetery, which was dedicated on June 6, 1866, is part of Mount Hebron Cemetery. It contains 3,423 Confederate dead. People throughout the South contributed funds to reinter the bodies and to erect monuments from each state. Ceremonies are still held every June 6, Confederate Memorial Day. Photo by Alan Lehman; courtesy of the Northern Virginia Daily

CHAPTER

6

Remembering

National Cemetery was established by the U.S. government, which purchased five acres along National Avenue in Winchester from Jacob Baker. Bodies within a twelve-mile radius were reinterred by Union troops occupying the area.

The cemetery contains 5,480 Union dead. Monuments were erected by the states of Ohio, Pennsylvania, Vermont, New Hampshire, New York, and Massachusetts to honor their fallen soldiers. American veterans who fought in subsequent wars, including Vietnam, also are buried there. Photo by Corinne R. Jervis; courtesy of the Winchester Star.

The Civil War brought sorrow, suffering, and devastation to Frederick County and the Northern Shenandoah Valley. Farms and houses were ravaged and people holding Confederate dollars found themselves broke. Husbands, fathers, sons, and brothers were killed and those who survived had to start over from scratch. It was a time of rebuilding, mourning, and remembering.

Not long after Gen. Robert E. Lee's surrender at Appomattox, local farmers preparing their fields for spring planting found themselves plowing up the remains of Confederate soldiers. Mary Dunbar Williams heard the grisly news, discussed it with her sister-in-law, Eleanor Williams Boyd, and together they organized the Ladies Confederate Memorial Association, which established Stonewall Cemetery.

On June 6, 1866, residents marked the opening of the cemetery and commemorated the anniversary of the death of Gen. Turner Ashby, who had been killed on Port Republic Road near Harrisonburg in 1862. First known as Turner Ashby Day, the anniversary was later celebrated as Confederate Memorial Day in Winchester and Harrisonburg.

In the years before the Shenandoah Apple Blossom Festival, Confederate Memorial Day was Winchester's largest annual event. The streets swelled with people who came to watch a parade, listen to speakers commemorate the dead, and lay flowers on the graves at Stonewall Cemetery.

The years after the war were also a time of occupation and unrest. Federal soldiers were garrisoned in Winchester until at least 1870. There was bitterness toward Northerners who had come to "reconstruct" the South and create a new civilian government. They were called carpetbaggers, and, according to Julia Davis in *The Shenandoah,* the *Winchester Times* defined them as "a two-legged animal of the male species which travels without a trunk, wears paper collars, and carries a great portion of his baggage on his back."

Edward Hall served in Company G, Thirtieth Regiment of the U.S. Colored Infantry. This photograph is of his tombstone in Orrick Cemetery on Valley Avenue in Winchester. Hall was born in Baltimore, Maryland, where he enlisted in March 1864. His unit was in the Battle of the Crater at Petersburg. He survived and became a sergeant in 1865. According to Winchester census records, he and his wife, Emma, lived in 1900 on Monmouth Street, where he worked as a gardener. There were black soldiers on both sides of the Civil War although obviously there were more who fought for the Union. Levi Miller, one of the few black Confederates, lived in Frederick County and died at Opequon in 1921. He served in Company C, Fifth Texas Regiment. Courtesy of Alan Tischler

The daughter of Capt. George W. Kurtz, Lucy Fitzhugh Kurtz was a charter member of the Turner Ashby Chapter, United Daughters of the Confederacy, when it formed in 1894. She also was president of the Stonewall Memorial Association, was responsible for the care of the graves at Stonewall Cemetery, and helped to compile a list of soldiers buried in the cemetery that was published in 1962. Born in 1872, "Miss Lucy" was the second woman in Winchester to obtain a driver's license. She was known throughout the community for her work to honor and assist Confederate veterans. This photograph was taken about 1900. She died in 1969. From the Stewart Bell Collection; courtesy of the Winchester-Frederick County Historical Society

The bronze Confederate infantryman's statue in front of the old Frederick County Courthouse was unveiled on November 15, 1916, by William P. McGuire and John Eddy. Harry St. George Tucker of Lexington, Virginia, former congressman of the Tenth District, spoke. The statue, still a downtown Winchester landmark, is seven and a half feet tall and stands on a base that is five and a half feet tall. Courtesy of the Winchester-Frederick County Historical Society

Valley Pike, now U.S. 11 south of Winchester, as it looked in 1885 looking north. Photo by James B. Wortham of Winchester, courtesy of the Massachusetts Military Order of the Loyal Legion of the United States, U.S. Army, Military History Institute, Carlisle Barracks, Pennsylvania

Confederate veteran Frederick William Mackey Holliday became governor of Virginia in 1878 and served one term. He advocated paying off debts the state had amassed before and during the Civil War and opposed the public school system that Virginia established in 1870, believing free schools were a luxury.

Holliday was born in 1828 in Winchester. He was a graduate of Yale University and had a law degree from the University of Virginia. He was only twenty-two when he was elected commonwealth's attorney for Winchester and Frederick County. He was a leader of local secessionist advocates.

Holliday commanded Company D of the Thirty-third Virginia Infantry of the Stonewall Brigade. He lost his right arm in 1862 at the Battle of Cedar Run and was called the sleeveless or one-armed hero of the Shenandoah Valley. From 1864 until the end of the war, he held Winchester's seat in the Confederate House of Representatives.

A Democrat, he ran unopposed for governor in 1877. His policies, including a move to raise personal property taxes by 80 percent, proved unpopular. Holliday returned to live in Winchester and bought Woodville, a large farm near Sunnyside. He died in 1889. Courtesy of the Handley Library Archives

An immigrant who fled Ireland's nineteenth-century potato famine, John Handley came to the United States, studied law, become a Pennsylvania judge, and made a fortune in real estate and mining anthracite coal. He shared his wealth with Winchester but never lived in the area.

Handley was born in 1835 and had received a limited education before immigrating to the United States in 1854. Upon his death in 1895, he left $250,000 for a public library. He also left the remainder of his estate in trust for twenty years and specified that it be used to build a school for the city's poor. As a result, the Handley Library was built in 1913; John Handley High School was built in 1923; and Douglas School, an all-black school, was built in 1927.

Handley, who lived in Scranton, Pennsylvania, enlisted in the Eighth Infantry Regiment of the state's militia during the Civil War but left after three months. He had strong Southern sympathies and became acquainted with Winchester while visiting a Scranton family that had moved to the area. He was impressed by people he met, including Confederate veterans such as Frederick W. M. Holliday, and bought a burial plot in Mount Hebron Cemetery that faced Stonewall Cemetery, where the area's Confederate soldiers are buried. Courtesy of the Winchester-Frederick County Historical Society

Winchester benefactor Charles Broadway Rouss made and lost two fortunes before his national chain of general merchandise stores made him a multimillionaire in the 1890s. He was a pioneer of the discount store and mail order house.

Born in Woodsboro, Maryland, in 1836, he moved with his family to Apple Pie Ridge in what is now Berkeley County, West Virginia. His first business experiences came from trading farm goods for staples at a country store at Whitehall and selling produce at the old markethouse in Winchester at the site of the city hall that now bears his name.

He opened his first general merchandise store at the site of Wilkins ShoeCenter. He lost his first fortune during the Civil War, despite success as a blockade runner, and enlisted as a Confederate private. After the war, he went to New York City, opened a chain of stores and amassed a second fortune, which he lost in the business panic of 1875. Undaunted, Rouss opened another chain and began a mail order business with a catalog he wrote using phonetic spelling.

Rouss began going blind in 1895 and died in 1902. He donated thirty thousand dollars each for the construction of Rouss City Hall and for the city's waterworks, ten thousand dollars for the castle-like building at the entrance of Mount Hebron Cemetery, and five thousand dollars each for Winchester Memorial Hospital and Rouss Fire Hall. He also paid for the iron fence around Mount Hebron and gave money for Rouss Hall at the University of Virginia, the Confederate Memorial Institute in Richmond, and, for New York City's Lafayette Park, a forty-five-foot bronze statue of Washington and Lafayette clasping hands. Courtesy of the Handley Library Archives

State Sen. S. Lucien Lupton (1854-1920) helped make Frederick County one of the nation's largest apple producers. His father, Dr. John S. Lupton, planted the first commercial apple orchard in Virginia west of the Blue Ridge Mountains. Lupton inherited his father's orchards and planted more. He also helped to organize growers and standardize the local apple industry by promoting uniform grading and containers. He helped form the Frederick County Fruit Growers Association and the Eastern Fruit Growers Association. Lupton, a Democrat, was elected to the Senate in 1900 and represented Winchester and Frederick and Shenandoah counties for four years. He later was appointed to the State Corporation Commission. He created the Lupton Horticultural Department at Handley High School. In 1919 Lupton sold his orchards for $250,000. Courtesy of the Winchester-Frederick County Historical Society

An ex-Confederate, Housan K. Pritchard
(1841-1920) turned to writing after the Civil
War. He and two other veterans, G. R. Henry
and P. L. Kurtz, established the Winchester
News, a weekly newspaper, in 1865. Pritchard
was its chief editorial writer through Reconstruc-
tion and until the newspaper was sold in 1898.

Pritchard, who was born on South Loudoun
Street in 1841, enlisted in the Confederate Army
before he was twenty and served from the First
Battle of Manassas until the end of the war. He
was a member of Marion's Rifles of the Stonewall Brigade and rose to the rank of first lieutenant. Courtesy of the Winchester-Frederick
County Historical Society

Josiah Thomas Walls, a free black man, was
born in Winchester in 1842 and moved to Florida. Drafted into the Confederate Army, Walls
joined the Union Army after being captured and
rose to the rank of sergeant-major. Upon his dis-
charge, he returned to Florida, where he became
a wealthy farmer and miller. He became a
member of the state legislature and was elected
to Florida's only seat in Congress in 1871, where
he served until 1876. Later he became farm
superintendent at Tallahassee State College,
now Florida A & M University. He died in
1905. Courtesy of the Florida State University

George Washington, the founder of Centralia, Washington, was born in Frederick County in 1817. The son of a slave, he was adopted by a white couple who took him to Missouri when they moved there. Washington, who had no formal schooling, operated a sawmill in St. Joseph. Faced with discrimination in Missouri, and later in Illionis, he and his adoptive parents in 1850 went west by wagon train to Oregon, where Washington became a lumberjack and helped his parents build a house. He staked a claim on 640 acres that later would become Centralia but had to put the land in his father's name because Oregon banned settlement by blacks. When the Northern Pacific Railroad was built through his property, Washington platted lots for a town. Economic depression hit in 1893, but Washington kept the town going by providing food and lending residents money without interest or terms of repayment. He died in 1905. Courtesy of Centralia College

Denver, Colorado, is named for Frederick County native James W. Denver. He was born in 1817 and lived until he was twenty-three at the farm of his father, Irish immigrant Patrick Denver, on Indian Hollow Road. James Denver was a surveyor and a teacher in Missouri and Kentucky before moving to Cincinnati, Ohio, in 1842 and studying law. He later moved to Trinity County, California, and was elected to the state legislature in 1851. While in office, he killed the editor of a San Francisco newspaper who challenged him to a duel; he also rescued more than one hundred immigrants stranded on their way to California. Denver became California's secretary of state in 1853 and was elected to Congress in 1855. Appointed commissioner of Indian affairs in 1857, he was sent to the Kansas Territory to make peace with the Indians. When Denver was later appointed governor of the territory, he quickly established law and order. Denver was named for him because he supported dividing Kansas into two states and suggested that one of them be named Colorado. He died in 1892. Courtesy of the Denver Public Library, Western History Department

Born near Brucetown in 1840, Charles Triplett O'Ferrall became governor of Virginia in 1893 and was the first chief executive to articulate the state's right-to-work philosophy. He grew up in Morgan County, West Virginia, was appointed clerk of the county court in 1855 at the age of fifteen, and was elected to the post two years later. O'Ferrall enlisted in the Confederate Army in 1861 and advanced to the rank of major. Wounded eight times, he was once left for dead. In 1865 he became commander of cavalry forces in the Shenandoah Valley.

After the war, O'Ferrell practiced law in Harrisonburg, was elected to represent Rockingham County in the House of Delegates in 1871, and later became a judge. He represented the Seventh District in Congress for six terms before resigning to become governor.

As governor, O'Ferrall promoted Virginia's economy and worked to resolve disputes with Maryland over boundaries and oyster fishing in the Chesapeake Bay. During an 1895 strike in southwest Virginia, he sent in troops to protect working miners. His effectiveness fell in 1896 when he took unpopular stands on national issues. He criticized the Democratic nominee for president, populist William Jennings Bryan, and was a staunch supporter of the gold monetary standard. O'Ferrall died in 1905. Courtesy of the Virginia State Library

William B. McKinley visited Winchester in May 1901, soon after his second inauguration and at the peak of his popularity. The last Civil War veteran to become president, McKinley had ties to Winchester. In May 1865, when he was a twenty-five-year-old Union Army captain, McKinley became a member of Winchester's Masonic Lodge at a building at Loudoun and Piccadilly streets, where Dominion Bank is now located.

McKinley served in the Twenty-third Ohio Volunteer Regiment under Col. Rutherford B. Hayes, who also became president. Both fought in the Second Battle of Winchester.

During his 1901 visit, McKinley promised to pay a return visit in September, but on September 6 he was shot by a young anarchist in Buffalo, New York, and died eight days later. Courtesy of the Winchester-Frederick County Historical Society

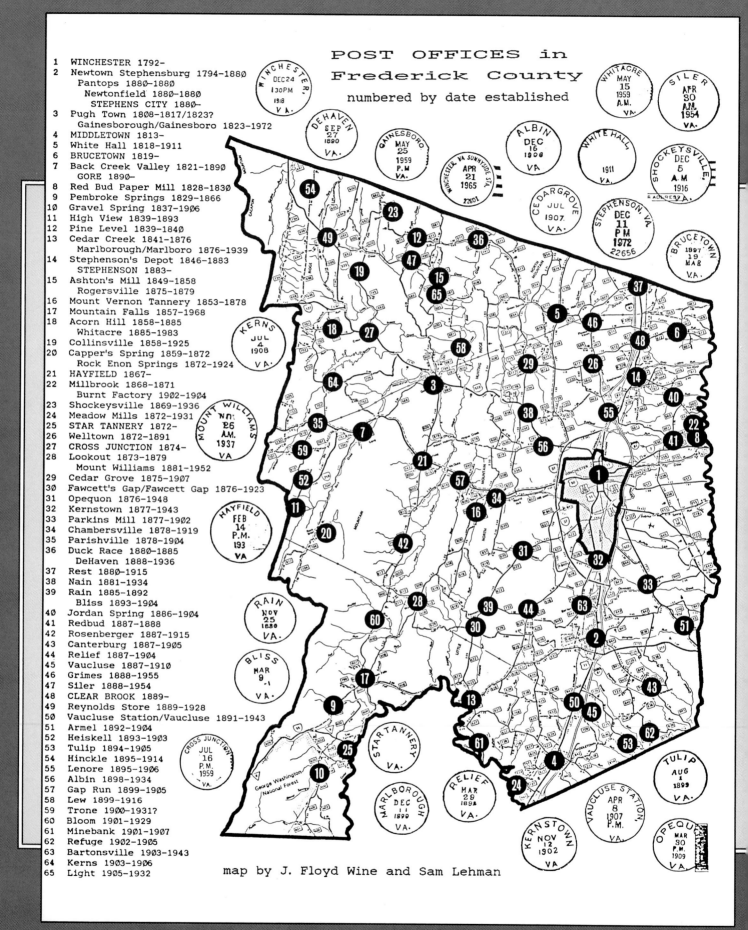

POST OFFICES in Frederick County
numbered by date established

1 WINCHESTER 1792-
2 Newtown Stephensburg 1794-1880
    Pantops 1880-1880
     Newtonfield 1880-1880
      STEPHENS CITY 1880-
3 Pugh Town 1808-1817/1823?
    Gainesborough/Gainesboro 1823-1972
4 MIDDLETOWN 1813-
5 White Hall 1818-1911
6 BRUCETOWN 1819-
7 Back Creek Valley 1821-1890
    GORE 1890-
8 Red Bud Paper Mill 1828-1830
9 Pembroke Springs 1829-1866
10 Gravel Spring 1837-1906
11 High View 1839-1893
12 Pine Level 1839-1840
13 Cedar Creek 1841-1876
    Marlborough/Marlboro 1876-1939
14 Stephenson's Depot 1846-1883
    STEPHENSON 1883-
15 Ashton's Mill 1849-1858
    Rogersville 1875-1879
16 Mount Vernon Tannery 1853-1878
17 Mountain Falls 1857-1968
18 Acorn Hill 1858-1885
    Whitacre 1885-1983
19 Collinsville 1858-1925
20 Capper's Spring 1859-1872
    Rock Enon Springs 1872-1924
21 HAYFIELD 1867-
22 Millbrook 1868-1871
    Burnt Factory 1902-1904
23 Shockeysville 1869-1936
24 Meadow Mills 1872-1931
25 STAR TANNERY 1872-
26 Welltown 1872-1891
27 CROSS JUNCTION 1874-
28 Lookout 1873-1879
    Mount Williams 1881-1952
29 Cedar Grove 1875-1907
30 Fawcett's Gap/Fawcett Gap 1876-1923
31 Opequon 1876-1948
32 Kernstown 1877-1943
33 Parkins Mill 1877-1902
34 Chambersville 1878-1919
35 Parishville 1878-1904
36 Duck Race 1880-1885
    DeHaven 1888-1936
37 Rest 1880-1915
38 Nain 1881-1934
39 Rain 1885-1892
    Bliss 1893-1904
40 Jordan Spring 1886-1904
41 Redbud 1887-1888
42 Rosenberger 1887-1915
43 Canterburg 1887-1905
44 Relief 1887-1904
45 Vaucluse 1887-1910
46 Grimes 1888-1955
47 Siler 1888-1954
48 CLEAR BROOK 1889-
49 Reynolds Store 1889-1928
50 Vaucluse Station/Vaucluse 1891-1943
51 Armel 1892-1904
52 Heiskell 1893-1903
53 Tulip 1894-1905
54 Hinckle 1895-1914
55 Lenore 1895-1906
56 Albin 1898-1934
57 Gap Run 1899-1905
58 Lew 1899-1916
59 Trone 1900-1931?
60 Bloom 1901-1929
61 Minebank 1901-1907
62 Refuge 1902-1905
63 Bartonsville 1903-1943
64 Kerns 1903-1906
65 Light 1905-1932

map by J. Floyd Wine and Sam Lehman

CHAPTER

7

Families and Communities

At the center of most older communities was the post office. Over the years there have been dozens of them in Frederick County. Many were operated at country stores or other businesses within communities. Today there are nine post offices in the county—Brucetown, Clearbrook, Cross Junction, Gore, Middletown, Star Tannery, Stephens City, Stephenson, and Hayfield—and two in Winchester—Pleasant Valley Road and the Loudoun Street Mall. There also are twenty-two rural routes and seven highway contract routes for delivering letters and packages to the mailboxes of county residents. Mail has been distributed in the city and county since colonial times. The area's first federal post office opened in Winchester on June 12, 1792, with merchant Daniel Norton as the postmaster. Local rural free delivery service was established in 1904.

Post Offices

Postmaster Charles Parish, Jr., raises the flag at the old Gore Post Office in 1957. From left to right are Huston Miller, Lloyd Elliot, Bill Dunlap, James Elliot, and Billy Dunlop. Courtesy of Grace Parish

James Henry Ritter was the postmaster of Welltown, which had a post office from 1872 to 1891. Ritter was born in 1854 and died in 1888. Courtesy of the Handley Library Archives

H. A. Funk was in charge of the new rural free delivery route through Stephens City, Vaucluse, Canterburg, and Marlboro beginning on August 1, 1904. He continued as a rural carrier until his retirement in 1932. His first means of transportation was a white mule named Jim Nate and the dog cart in this photograph dated circa 1915. It was taken by one of the patrons along his route. Courtesy of Martha E. Funk

Frederick County is a patchwork of families and communities and the post offices, schools, churches, and country stores that have grown up around them.

Frederick County is the towns of Stephens City and Middletown; the villages of Gainesboro, Gore, and Star Tannery; places, such as Stephenson, Marlboro, Whitehall, Grimes, Green Spring, Mt. Williams, and Mountain Falls; and communities within communities, such as Mudville and Freetown at Stephens City.

Communities are places called home and families are the reason they are called home. They are nostalgic hamlets of the past and the subdivisions of today. They are places where people lived or grew up. They are places where ancestors forged a future for the generations to come. Homes are places that are never forgotten and families are people who are never far from the heart.

Wagonmaking was a thriving business in nineteenth-century Stephens City. During the period of the California Gold Rush, the town had thirteen shops producing wagons, such as the one in this 1920 photograph. Called Newtown wagons, they were known for their sturdiness. From the John Walter Wayland Collection; courtesy of the Winchester-Frederick County Historical Society

Stephens City

Known over the years as Stephens Town, Stephensburg, Newtown, and Pantops, Stephens City is the second oldest town in Frederick County. It was named for its founder, Lewis Stephens, and was chartered as Stephensburg by the General Assembly in September 1758. Another legislative act on October 12, 1758, established the town on nine hundred acres that Stephens owned.

Stephens was the son of Peter Stephens, a German Lutheran immigrant who first settled in Germantown, Pennsylvania. Their family was among the first band of pioneers who came to Frederick County with Jost Hite in 1732. The younger Stephens operated a mill and began an ironworks at Marlboro that he later sold to Isaac Zane, Jr. Stephens was appointed a militia captain in 1753 and promoted to major in 1757.

Stephens City, the name given the town by the legislature in May 1887, was called Newtown earlier in the nineteenth century when the town was extended northward. The new section was called Newtown and the name gradually became used for the entire town.

Over the years, Stephens City has been a commercial and industrial center and a major crossroads. At the center of town was the intersection of a road that led to Alexandria (now State Route 277) and another that went to Knoxville, Tennessee (the forerunner of U.S. 11 and Interstate 81). Known for its wagonmakers, the town did

a booming business from pioneers heading west. In the early twentieth century, a business center known as Mudville sprang up around the limestone quarry and lime kiln that opened on the west side of town.

Today the area east of Stephens City is one of the fastest growing sections of Frederick County. With Interstate 81 only a block from the town limits, and its junction with Interstate 66 just a few miles away near Middletown, continued development is assured. The town's population was 606 in 1940 and had reached 876 by 1960. It declined to 802 in 1970 but grew to 1,179 in 1980, an increase of 47 percent over ten years, and is projected to reach between 1,255 and 1,429 by 1990 and 1,367 and 1,696 by the year 2000.

Within residential subdivisions such as Fredericktowne, the Pines, and Greenbrier Village, the Opequon District that surrounds Stephens City had one of the fastest growth rates in Frederick County from 1970 to 1980, when it grew by 56 percent.

The Newtown Tavern at 5408 Main Street, shown in this 1916 photograph, has a rich past. Constructed in 1819, it stood at a major cross-roads (now State Route 277 and U.S. 11). Wagon drivers used to open their bedrolls before the fireplace in the barroom and spend the night. One overnight guest of note was Gen. Philip Sheridan.

Another notable guest was Andrew Jackson, seventh president of the United States. Among the townspeople gathered at the tavern to see him was a small boy who exclaimed, "Why, he is just a man." Jackson, the self-proclaimed champion of the common man, told the boy he was right and went on to give a speech.

The Newtown Tavern is now owned by attorney Lewis M. Costello, whose son-in-law and daughter, Jonathan and Lyda Bitto, have converted it into a bed and breakfast inn. Courtesy of Joy and Lewis Costello

Although born in Winchester as a slave, the Rev. Robert Orrick became the richest black man in town and the black community's first minister. Once owned by Major Kean, a clerk of the Circuit Court, Orrick was allowed to operate a business even while still a slave. He owned livery stables on Cecil and Washington streets and two farms in Frederick County. He also had government contracts to carry mail from Winchester to Rock Enon Springs, Marlboro, and Cedar Creek in Virginia and Romney and Bloomery, West Virginia. An ordained minister in the African Methodist Episcopal Church, he built Orrick Chapel at Stephens City at his own expense and donated land for Orrick Cemetery, a black cemetery on Valley Avenue. At the time of his death in 1902, Orrick lived at 15 South Braddock Street in Winchester. Courtesy of the Handley Library

Stephens City once had a jail at 216 Main Street, where the Farmers & Merchants National Bank branch is now. This photograph was taken circa 1890. Courtesy of Louise Stover Brim

Charles Sandy Headley, a well-known Stephens City carpenter born in 1873, posed with his bicycle around the turn of the century. Photo by Davidson Brothers of Winchester, an early portrait studio at the Masonic Temple on Loudoun Street. Courtesy of Headley's granddaughter, Ann Stimmel

Mary Mollie McCarty Craig lived west of Stephens City. She and her husband, William O. Craig, had five sons. She died in 1913. Courtesy of Alice, her granddaughter, and Oren Snapp

Elmer Steele, a Stephens City dentist, went on a picnic with three ladies in 1899. From left to right are his sister, Cara Steele Grove, Mamie Coffman Fetzer of Woodstock, and Katie Staling of Harrisonburg. Courtesy of Cara Grove's daughter, Mildred Lee Grove

Early twentieth-century travelers did not get past the tollbooth, shown above, on Valley Pike (now U.S. 11) at the northern end of Stephens City without first paying tollkeeper Jim Painter (standing alone). The man driving the pony cart was Waldo Hack. The women have not been identified. Photos courtesy of Louise Stover Brim

The lime plant has been a Stephens City landmark throughout this century. It is on State Route 631, the Lime Kiln Road. The kiln in this 1939 photograph was the original one for the M. J. Grove Lime Company, based in Frederick, Maryland, which began a quarry and kiln operation in 1902 after rich veins of high-quality limestone were discovered. The lime plant became the community's main industry. A nearby barrel factory was established to meet the kiln's needs, and Stephens City got electricity when a line to the lime plant was extended from the Shenandoah River.

Flintkote Corporation bought the plant and quarry about 1960; about 1980, Genstar Stone Products Company bought the business but gave up the quarry operation because of the high cost of pumping water from underground streams. James L. Bowman bought the property in 1983 but Genstar was allowed to continue to process hydrated lime through September 1988. The lime is used for sewage treatment, water purification, agriculture, and industrial uses, such as the manufacture of paint, plastics, and glass. Courtesy of Genstar Stone Products Company

Mudville along Lime Kiln Road was a thriving industrial and commercial village west of downtown Stephens City. It never fully recovered from the Great Depression and a devastating 1936 fire. This building, razed in 1985, once housed a general store, a train station, and a telegraph office. It stood on the north side of State Route 277, across from the lime kiln. People who lived and worked in Mudville said children used to play outside while their fathers parked the family's horses and carriages and their mothers shopped. Farmers brought eggs and butter to exchange for dry goods. There was a flour mill, an apple-drying plant, the farmer's supply co-operative, and a blacksmith shop. Around the turn of the century James Gardner operated a general store in the building but by 1909 had sold it to C. E. Staples. Gardner's son, Crowell, bought the business back from Staples in the early 1930s. Around 1945 James W. Golladay bought the building and operated his building supply company there until he moved up the road about 1970. Photo by Rick Foster; courtesy of the Winchester Star

The Redmen of Stephens City, a fraternal order, posed for this photograph taken about 1910 to 1915. Courtesy of the Handley Library Archives

Children and members of the International Order of the Oddfellows marched down Fairfax Street on Decoration Day, June 14, 1925. They are headed toward Green Hill Cemetery to decorate graves with flowers. Courtesy of Glen Combs

The Stephens City Lions Club was chartered on October 22, 1946. From left are Dr. Charles Anderson, Dr. Allen Hawthorne, Bev Cather, district governor Kenneth Cruser, and club president James W. Golladay, Sr. This photograph was taken during a banquet at the old Sarah Zane Fire Hall at North Loudoun Street and Fairfax Lane in Winchester. Courtesy of James W. Golladay, Jr

A great-great-great-great-granddaughter of Frederick County settler Peter Stephens, the Rev. Mary Louise Steele was a pioneer in her own right. She became one of the first female ministers of the United Methodist Church when she was licensed to preach in 1956 through the Braddock Street United Methodist Church in Winchester. By 1963, she was one of only seven female ministers in Virginia. There were more than 150 when she died in 1986.

Born in Stephens City in 1902, Steele was an honor graduate of Handley High School and attended Madison College, Shenandoah College and Conservatory, and the University of Virginia. Besides being a minister, she also was an accountant, a teacher, and a nurse. She spent more than ten years as a minister in the Winchester District of the Methodist Church and later accepted ministerial appointments in Rappahannock County, Danville, Staunton, Mt. Olive, and Lynchburg, as well as on the Eastern Shore. Courtesy of Helen Rinker Snapp

S. Mason Carbaugh was appointed Virginia's commissioner of agriculture in 1972 by Gov. Linwood Holton and has been reappointed by each succeeding governor through Gerald L. Baliles. He was born on a farm west of Stephens City and grew up there and at another farm at Bartonsville. He is a graduate of Stephens City High School and Virginia Tech.

Carbaugh taught vocational agriculture and worked as a feed sales representative for the Quaker Oats Company before going to work for the state in 1961 as a specialist in marketing and transporting farm products and supplies. He later was director of the Virginia Soil and Water Conservation Board and was executive director of the Commission of the Industry of Agriculture. Photo by Dementi-Foster Studios, courtesy of the Virginia Department of Agriculture

83

Stephens City native Mildred Lee Grove donated the stone building at 5428 Main Street to Frederick County in 1987 for a local history museum. The building, which she had owned since 1930, was constructed about 1761. Photo by Teresa Lazazzera

Teacher and local historian Mildred Lee Grove in 1986 became one of the first people in the United States to receive a national community service award from the American Association of Retired Persons. In 1987, she was the first person named historian of the year by the Winchester-Frederick County Historical Society. A Stephens City native, Miss Grove taught English at Handley High School from 1925 to 1949 and was a visiting teacher for Winchester schools until her retirement in 1968. It was her job to contact students who were not attending school and work with parents and social agencies to get them back into the classroom. The retired teachers and school administrators who nominated her for the community service award said she also helped provide books and clothing for children. Courtesy of the Winchester Star

The municipal offices of Stephens City were dedicated on September 9, 1979. Before moving there, the town offices had been in several spots, including the old Stephens City School. Photo by Alan Lehman; courtesy of the Northern Virginia Daily

Postal carriers John Petrie, left, and Julian Carbaugh, taking out the mail at the old Stephens City post office on Main Street in 1980. It was replaced in 1981 by a modern facility on the north end of town. Photo by Larry Sullivan; courtesy of the Winchester Star

Cornelia Barbour Turner Avery, a midwife, learned how to deliver children from her mother, Emily Robinson Barbour. Avery was born in 1867 east of Stephens City. She had eight children, including Ethel Williams, who also is pictured on this page, and raised a number of foster children. Known as "Aunt Neely," Avery walked many miles to aid women who were about to give birth or traveled by horse and buggy or automobile to the homes of her more affluent patients. She also did housework for local families, was the superintendent of Orrick Chapel, and was a member of the Loving Charity Lodge, a black organization that helped the needy. Known for her expertise in making sausage and apple butter, neighbors often sought her help at butchering and harvest time. She died in 1943. Courtesy of Ethel Williams

Ethel Williams stands in front of the house where she was born in 1901 at Freetown, a black community east of Stephens City. The house was the home of her mother, Cornelia Avery, and her grandparents. Williams said the community on State Route 641 used to be known as Crossroads, which may have come from the nearby intersection of State Route 277 and Double Churches Road. Nine black families, including Robinsons, Washingtons, Lewises, Dormans, and Dunns, used to live there years before the road was paved and while cars were still a rarity. A few families still remain, including Williams' sons, Lawrence and Jimmy Williams. Williams left Crossroads when she was twelve and has lived most of her life in Stephens City and Winchester. She has cleaned houses, looked after children, and washed and ironed clothes for others. Photo by Rick Foster; courtesy of the Winchester Star

Middletown

Originally known as Senseney Town, Middletown was chartered on May 3, 1796, by its founder, Dr. Peter Senseney, and his wife, Magdalin. Because the new community was halfway between Stephens City (then called Newtown), which was five miles north, and Strasburg (then called Stover), which was five miles south, it became known as Middletown.

Senseney, a German settler from Pennsylvania, also had a home on East Cork Street in Winchester and is the person for whom Senseny Road is named, despite the difference in spelling.

Senseney is credited with requiring houses in the town to be built well off the main street, which later became Valley Pike and today is U.S. 11. When the road was widened in the 1930s, Middletown was one of few towns along the highway that did not have to move houses to make way for construction.

Middletown has long enjoyed a reputation as a cultural and educational center. Jacob Danner and Anthony Kline were making clocks, watches, and surveying instruments there as early as 1786. A tavern that became the Wayside Inn on Main Street was built in 1797 and remains a popular tourist stop. Just south of town is Belle Grove Plantation, a restored eighteenth-century mansion and estate that now is operated as a musuem by the National Trust for Historic Preservation. The surrounding countryside was the scene of the Battle of Cedar Creek, fought on October 18, 1864.

Late in the nineteenth century, the Shenandoah Normal School operated at the present site of Wayside Theatre on Main Street. Middletown School, built in 1909, was the first high school in Frederick County and the first agricultural school in Virginia. Today, Lord Fairfax Community College is on U.S. 11 just north of town.

Middletown was incorporated in 1878 and J. W. Rhodes was elected the first mayor. In 1889 more than two thousand lots were added to the town and platted in anticipation of a land boom that never materialized. The town, nevertheless, grew, from 156 people in 1800 to 423 in 1900. By 1980 there were 841 people, an addition of 334 people since 1970 or an increase of nearly 66 percent. Part of the reason for the increase was the annexation of eighty-six acres at the end of 1978, which boosted the town's size to 429 acres. Located north of the junction of Interstates 81 and 66, the town is expected to have a population of fifteen hundred people by 2020.

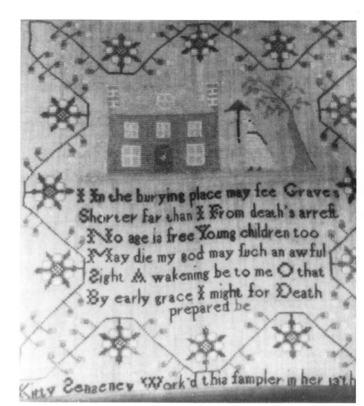

Katherine Senseney, daughter of Middletown founder Peter Senseney, sewed this sampler in 1804 when she was thirteen. Courtesy of Phil Whitney

George Bell, a convert of John Wesley, brought Methodism to Middletown in the early nineteenth century. The congregation that became Grace United Methodist Church first met in a log cabin built in 1820 for use by all denominations. The Methodists used the log cabin until 1852, when a brick church was built across from the current church on Main Street. The church, designed in a modified Queen Anne style, was built in 1894 through public contributions and donated labor. It was dedicated on July 30, 1898, with twelve hundred people attending; an estimated twenty-five hundred people visited the church throughout the day. The church became Grace United Methodist when the Methodists and the United Brethren combined in 1968. Photo by Ray K. Saunders; courtesy of the Winchester Star

Wrecked during the Civil War and neglected during the early twentieth century, St. Thomas Chapel in Middletown has since been restored to its antebellum splendor. Land for the church was purchased in 1834 and the building, originally called the St. Thomas Episcopal Church, was constructed by 1836. The church design was based on a portion of York Cathedral in northern England. During the Civil War, the church was taken over by both Confederate and Union troops and was used as a hospital and a stable. Parishioners began rebuilding after the war and installed the church's four-tiered chandelier. They applied to the federal government for wartime damages, and in 1904 they received just $1,004. Over the years the congregation dwindled, and the church closed in 1946. Deeded to Middletown in 1967, the church was restored through an $11,000 grant from the National Park Service in 1974, with matching funds raised from donations and events such as bake sales and ice cream socials. Now listed on the state and national registers of historic places, St. Thomas is today an interfaith chapel used for weddings and special ceremonies at holidays. The 1974 photo by David Newlin, was taken before restoration began; the photo by Scott Mason shows the restored chapel in 1987. Courtesy of the Winchester Star

The Middletown Town Hall was built about 1880 and was used as a public school until 1908. The building was deeded to the town in 1912 with the stipulation that the International Order of Odd Fellows be allowed to use the top floor for meetings and use the lower floor at least six times a year for community events. In 1965, IOOF deeded its interest in the building to the town. The building also has housed the town fire department. Photo by Teresa Lazazzera

The Wayside Inn as it looked in the early 1900s and as it looks today. A premier Shenandoah Valley tourist stop, the inn has been operating since 1797. It was first called Wilkerson's Tavern and was renamed Larrick's Hotel when Jacob Larrick bought it after the Civil War. Its current name came in the twentieth century. Samuel Rhodes, a more recent owner, also added a third floor and wings on each side of the building and, with the advent of automo-

J. P. Cadwallader of Fredericktowne peruses a May 26, 1909, issue of the Middletown Mirror that he bought for two dollars at Greg DeLoach's auction house in Stephens City in 1987. The issue contained an item about his mother: "Mrs. Emma Cadwallader has been quite sick but is much better now." Cadwallader, who was born three months later, believes his mother must have been suffering from morning sickness. Another important story in that issue is the cornerstone-laying ceremony for the old Middletown School. Ads in the paper show that a dozen eggs sold for eighteen cents, and sodas sold for five cents each. Photo by Rick Foster; courtesy of the Winchester Star

biles, dubbed Wayside "America's First Motor Inn." Leo Bernstein, a Washington banker and financier, bought the inn in 1960 and refurbished it. Gutted by a fire on the morning of October 3, 1985, it reopened in September 1986 after extensive repairs and renovation. Earlier photo courtesy of Louise Stover Brim; recent photo by Alan Lehman, courtesy of the Northern Virginia Daily

The Middletown Agricultural High School, which opened on October 4, 1909, was Virginia's first agricultural school and Frederick County's first high school. This is a photograph of the school's students in 1915. It opened with 190 elementary and high school students and offered classes in agriculture, manual training, woodworking, and cooking. It was built without tax money through monetary donations by local people and donated labor and supplies. It operated as a high school until 1950 and as an elementary school until 1984. According to the May 26, 1909 issue of the Middletown Mirror, about two thousand people traveled by bicycle, foot, buggy, carriage, rail, and automobile to witness the laying of the school's cornerstone. Sen. Ronald M. Ward and Willet M. Hayes, assistant secretary of the U.S. Department of Agriculture, addressed the crowd. Courtesy of Ruby E. Campbell

Members of the Middletown Elementary School Parent-Teacher Association and the Town Council, youngsters, and a dog named Lucky are shown here demonstrating in opposition to the closing of the school, shown in the rear. Councilwoman Eleanor Coverstone is on the far right holding an SOS sign and Councilman Joseph Carper is on the far right, sitting on the stone fence. The school was closed in 1984 despite protests, petitions, and emotional pleas from alumni and local residents to keep it open. Residents cited the school's small student-teacher ratio and strong community support as reasons for not closing it. But school administrators pointed to maintenance problems and energy inefficiency and said money could be saved by closing the school. Formerly an agricultural high school, the building was seventy-five years old when it was closed, making it the oldest county school building still in operation at the time. After the school closed, students at other elementary schools were shifted to make room for Middletown students at Bass-Hoover Elementary School in Stephens City. Construction of an elementary school for six-hundred pupils began in 1988 just north of Lord Fairfax Community College. Photos by Scott Mason; courtesy of the Winchester Star

In the early twentieth century, J. I. Stover operated this flour and feed mill on the north end of Middletown, west of Main Street near the railroad tracks. The photograph was taken about 1920. The mill later burned. Courtesy of Stover's daughter, Louise Stover Brim

Everything from shoes to constipation-relieving "liver berries" (front left) could be bought at Edward R. Sperry's general store in Middletown. Sperry is the man standing behind the counter in this 1927 photograph. Ernest Funk is seated at the center left, just visible behind the displays. Courtesy of the Middletown Town Office

The Wayside Theatre in Middletown, the oldest resident summer stock theater in Virginia, celebrated its twenty-seventh season in 1988. It is one of only a few small-town repertory theaters that have hung on in an age of easy long-distance travel. The building, at Main and Second streets, was constructed in the mid 1940s by Herschel C. Borden and his son, George Wilson Borden, who operated a movie theater there. What now is the box office was then a soda fountain. A small store was in the section of the building that now houses the restaurant Curtain Call. The theater had its first season of production in 1962 when it was opened as Maralarrick Inc. Leo Bernstein, the owner of the Wayside Inn, bought the building in 1963 and changed the name to Wayside Theatre. Incorporated as a nonprofit foundation in 1966, the two-hundred-seat theater relies on ticket sales, donations, and grants to operate. Photo by Teresa Lazazzera

Calvin Gant, Sr., and his wife, Gladys Gant, are shown here in 1946 in front of the couple's home on Fourth Street in Middletown. They were married in 1938 and had four children. Calvin Gant was born in Stephenson and worked at the M. J. Grove Lime Company in Stephens City for thirty-one years. Gladys Gant was born in Warren County. Courtesy of Calvin and Gladys Gant

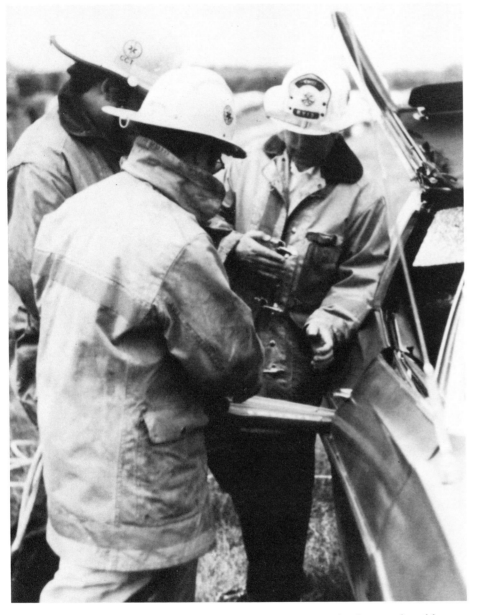

A Vietnam veteran and former Social Security administrator, Donald E. Ratcliff is chairman of the Frederick County 250th Anniversary Commission and president of the Shenandoah Apple Blossom Festival for 1989 and 1990. He lives just south of Middletown. Ratcliff was born in Tazewell County in 1936 and has a bachelor's degree in business administration from Concord College of Athens, West Virginia. As a Marine, he saw active duty in Southeast Asia and was later in the Marine Reserves. He is now a Realtor for Century 21 Plaza Real Estate in Winchester. Ratcliff also is a pilot and colonel in the Virginia Civil Air Patrol and was the organization's state commander from 1983 to 1985. As a qualified search and rescue pilot, he has found three crashed airplanes. Ratcliff was president of the Winchester Host Lions Club from 1978 to 1979. Courtesy of Donald Ratcliff

A rescue team from the Middletown Volunteer Fire Company and Rescue Squad is shown using the Jaws of Life, an extracting tool, to pry open the door of a wrecked car. The fire company organized in 1942, and the rescue squad formed in 1952. Today there are about fifty volunteers, about thirty-two of whom respond to calls. The company has two paid employees. Courtesy of Larry A. Oliver

Springdale, a stone mansion on the east side of U.S. 11 at Bartonsville (north of Stephens City), was built by Col. John Hite in 1753. His father, pioneer Jost Hite, built an earlier house southeast of Springdale and its ruins remain today. John Hite, Jr., who built Belle Grove, conveyed Springdale to David Brown, and Brown's heirs sold it in 1802 to Richard P. Barton, for whom the area is named. John Hite was a justice of the county in 1748, a militia colonel, and county lieutenant in 1776. His friend, future president George Washington, visited Springdale in 1748 after stopping at Jost Hite's Tavern. During Gen. Philip Sheridan's 1864 campaign, the mansion was used as a headquarters for Gen. William Dwight, a commander of Sheridan's Corps.

mander of Sheridan's Corps.

Springdale is shown here in a photograph dated July 11, 1873. On the lawn, left to right: Archibald Stuart Baldwin; Bolling Walker Barton; R. F. Harrison, and his wife Caroline Harrison, who bought the house that year from the executors of David Walker Barton's estate; Moffat (full name unknown); a nurse holding Randolph Jones Barton, Jr.; Randolph Jones Barton; and Uncle Isaac, a former slave of David Walker Barton. On the porch: Frances Jones Barton Marshall Holt, mother of the movie star Charles John "Jack" Holt; Mrs. Bolling Walker Barton; Margaret Lewis Marshall Duir; Mrs. David Walker Barton; and Mrs. Randolph Jones Barton; Courtesy of Ann L.B. Brown

The Bartonsville Mill still stands west of U.S. 11 south of Winchester and across from Springdale. It was built in 1788 at the site of an earlier mill constructed by settler Jost Hite. Once a well-known flour mill, it now is on the National Register of Historic Places. Courtesy of Martha Funk

These Stephens City men went on an outing at Crooked Run in 1894. Charles Frazier is on the far left and Lee Chipley is standing. William S. Rosenberger is seated and wearing a hat and Joe McCarty is on the far right. Harry Frazier, center, is fishing. Courtesy of Mildred Lee Grove

Shown here is the interior of the old St. Paul's Lutheran Church at Fawcett's Gap on Cedar Creek Grade. The church was built in 1856 on land donated by Henry Snapp; a few years later it was damaged by Union troops during the Civil War. The existing church was built in 1902. Courtesy of Virginia C. Fawcett and Evelyn Bywaters Goode

Daniel C. Funkhouser and his wife, Sarah Catherine Hersberger Funkhouser, lived at Fawcett's Gap on Cedar Creek Grade. Funkhouser was a Confederate soldier. The couple were married on January 28, 1873, and this photograph was taken soon after. Courtesy of their granddaughter, Marie Bowman

Members of the Fawcett family about 1895 at their home near St. Paul's Lutheran Church at Fawcett's Gap. The elderly couple seated in the front are Elkanah Fawcett and Margaret Funkhouser Fawcett, who were married in 1846. The man at the far left is identified only as Peffitt. Clarkson Thomas Fawcett is seated with his son, Lewis Ginn Fawcett. Gertie Crabill Tevalt is behind the fence. John William Marker is in front of the gate and behind his father-in-law, Elkanah. William Penn Fawcett is standing behind the fence on Marker's right. The little boy at the extreme right is believed to be Harry Elkanah Marker. Elkanah's parents, Joseph and Mary Branson Fawcett, built the stone house in 1790. They were Quakers. Courtesy of Lucy Fawcett Lamp

The family of Samuel and Margaret Cooper pose in 1894 at their home on Cedar Creek on State Route 714. From left to right, front row: John Lonas Heishman, Roy Heishman, Earl Samuel Cooper, Ernest Townes Cooper, Carroll Zepp, Guy Zepp, Lillian Zepp, and Maude Zepp. Middle row: Sanford Romanus Heishman, Percy Heishman, Virginia Catherine Cooper Heishman, Fred Heishman, John Henry Adam Cooper, John Cecil Cooper, Louisa Townes Cooper, Henry Harold Cooper, Albert Zepp, Mary Magdeline Cooper Zepp, and Frank E. Zepp. Back row: Margaret Catherine Heishman, Effie Heishman, Margaret Rudolph Cooper, and Samuel Cooper. Courtesy of Esther Cooper Moore

Joseph "Dody" Snapp was fit as a fiddle on his ninety-second birthday on June 27, 1944. A farmer, he lived on Cedar Creek Grade. He was born in 1852 and died in 1946. He and his wife, Martha Richard Snapp, had three children. Courtesy of Oren and Alice Snapp

Many a horse and carriage and early automobile that traveled Middle Road crossed the Marlboro Bridge over Cedar Creek. This photograph is dated 1922. The bridge burned in the 1930s. From the John Walter Wayland Collection; courtesy of the Winchester-Frederick County Historical Society

Jimmy Smith's Park on Cedar Creek near Marlboro was a favorite recreation spot for picnics, boating, fishing, and swimming. Thelma Racey and her brother-in-law, Paul Beatty, are shown playing horseshoes in this 1946 photograph. Courtesy of Paul and Garnette Beatty

Members of the Relief United Methodist Church pose in front of their church on Middle Road about 1914. Those identified include from left, front row: Cecil Elliott (second) and Floyd Snapp (third); second row: Alfred Snapp, Sr., George Snapp, Mabel Elliott, Dorothy Beatty Connor, Dovie Brown, Nannie Copenhaver Wigginton, and Ella Brown; third row: Mrs. Will Neikirk, Gertie Craig (mother of Alice Craig Snapp), Mildred Massie Branner, Benjamin Massie, Emily Massie Martin, Mary Massie Dorsey, Ida Mae Beatty Bennington, and Frances Beatty Broy; fourth row: Mrs. Brown with baby, the next three women and child not identified, Edna Snapp, Nannie Branner Womeldorph, and Gertie Snapp; fifth row: Mrs. Ashby Graves, Hattie Bassett Beatty, Genevieve Massie and William Neikirk; back row: Maynard Wisecarver, Russell Carpenter, a Mr. Barb, and Harvy Hicks. Courtesy of Oren and Alice Snapp

Known throughout the South for her culinary skills, Susan Josephine Tokes (1874-1955) operated the Tokes Inn off Cedar Creek Grade at Opequon. For more than thirty years Tokes, known as "Aunt Sue" and "Miss Sue," catered the Byrd picnics, premier political events of the time that drew Richmond and Washington legislators to the orchard of U.S. Sen. Harry F. Byrd, Sr. Tokes also catered the queen's luncheons of the Shenandoah Apple Blossom Festival for twenty-five years.

She began her catering career by serving a Red Cross dinner during World War I. Among the honors she received was a U.S. Treasury Department citation, presented in 1944 when she prepared her famous Southern fried chicken dinner in Winchester, Massachusetts, for the War Finance Program, which sold bonds to finance the war. The Virginia and Massachusetts Winchesters at the time were friendly rivals in selling war bonds. Tokes was also interviewed by the food editor of the Philadelphia Bulletin Sunday Magazine for a story that carried her photograph and several recipes. She was more than eighty years old when she appeared on the Ruth Crane television program in 1954 and shared recipes that she used in the Apple Blossom Festival. Courtesy of Mary Davis Byrd

Members of the Tokes, Byrd, Davis, and Turner families of Opequon are seen here in the late 1950s. From left, front: Addie Davis, Cecily Byrd Haston, Harmon Byrd, Jr., and Mary Davis Byrd. Middle row: Louisa Tokes Davis, George Christie, and Susan J. Tokes. Back row: George Davis, Esther Turner, and Harmon Byrd, Sr.

Louisa Davis and Susan Tokes were sisters.

Today, Addie Davis, Louisa Davis's daughter, still operates Tokes Inn, her aunt's well-known business. George Davis is Addie Davis's husband and George Christie is Addie's father. Esther Turner is Louisa Davis's sister-in-law. Mary Davis Byrd, also a daughter of Louisa Davis, is pictured with her husband, Harmon, and their children, Cecily and Harmon, Jr. Courtesy of Mary Davis Byrd

Four first cousins from the Stephens City area made up the Cousins Quartet, a gospel music singing group. This photograph was taken at Refuge United Methodist Church, where they performed June 18, 1950, when an addition to the church was opened. From left are Nancy Klem, Avis Petty, Claude Bennington, and Jackie White.

Refuge church and other churches named Fairview (State Route 641) and Relief (State Routes 628 and 629) trace their roots to the Rev. Frank A. Strother, a builder of Methodist churches. In 1889, he held a seven-week outdoor meeting that attracted people for miles. It was held at Fairfield, also known as "Lost Corner." Strother decided that the site, at State Routes 640 and 639, should no longer be called Lost Corner and instead should be the location of "a church of refuge" for the people. Courtesy of Dorothy Conner

Mary L. "Settie" Lowe, ninety-two gets a hug from her daughter, Eva Bly, sixty-seven, in this 1987 photograph in front of Lowe's house on State Route 629 west of Stephens City. When Lowe and her husband, John, moved to the house, in 1934, it had no electricity and water had to be carried from a spring. Photo by Rick Foster; courtesy of the Winchester Star

Mr. and Mrs. Joseph Miller at Wheatland, their home on the west side of U.S. 522 south of Winchester. The photograph was taken in the early 1900s. Courtesy of Frances C. Jett

William Ritter and his wife, Margaret Carper Ritter, pose on the front porch of their home on Parkins Mill Road about 1925. They were married on September 3, 1867. Courtesy of George L. Madigan, their grandson

Anne Fleming Judy, five, and her brother, Charles A. Fleming, nine, pose at the farm of their grandfather, O. H. Anderson, on Senseny Road in 1937. On the right is Pete Peacemaker, a young farmhand. Courtesy of Bill Madigan

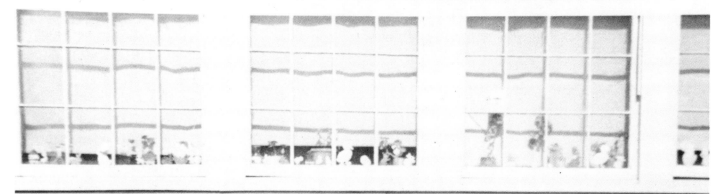

SOIL and LIFE IS YOUR FARMING ON THE LEVEL ON THE CONTOUR LORD FAIRFAX SOIL CONSERVATION DISTRICT

These are the students at Highview School circa 1950. Nellie Painter Coffelt, on the right, taught there many years and often had four grades at a time in the one-room schoolhouse, which then did not have indoor plumbing and was heated by a potbellied stove. The school, in southeastern Frederick County, closed in 1970. Courtesy of Paul and Garnette Beatty

Members of Ridings Chapel on Salem Church Road at the church's annual homecoming in 1978. From left to right: Frances Beatty Broy, who died in 1979, Mildred Hammock, Grace Beatty Evans, Edna Cadwallader, and Dorothy Beatty Conner. Courtesy of Dorothy Beatty Conner

Rebecca Lupton Funk Hallett peeling apples at her home on U.S. 11 south of Kernstown. She later dried the apples and used them in pies. The photograph was taken in the 1970s when she was about sixty-eight. Courtesy of Rebecca Lupton Funk Hallett

Gore

The village of Gore, which was earlier called Lockhart and the Back Creek Valley Post Office, is named for Sidney Sophia Cather Gore. It was part of a nineteenth-century timber paradise and resort area that was once known as the Back Creek Valley. Mrs. Gore's niece, Pulitzer Prize-winning novelist Willa Cather, was born and spent part of her childhood there before moving to Nebraska.

Jeremiah Smith was northwestern Frederick County's pioneer settler. He staked a claim north of Gore, at Bywater Spring on the banks of Back Creek, in the early 1730s. About twenty years later, in 1752, he returned from New Jersey with his second wife, Elizabeth.

Smith was born in 1711. He had 1,113 acres in Back Creek Valley and four hundred acres on Timber Ridge. The land was passed down to his children and grandchildren and was subdivided into other farms. Willa Cather's grandfather, William Cather, eventually bought some of the land on the original tract and built "Willow Shade."

In the years that followed, nearby Rock Enon and Capon Springs became thriving resorts. Timber also became Back Creek's major industry, and sawmills sprang up to provide wood for everything from barrels to railroad ties. The Winchester & Western Railroad came through in the 1920s, offering passenger service between Winchester and Wardensville, West Virginia, and a faster means for transporting timber to market. Unimin, a sandmining operation at Gore, continues to use the tracks today.

Gore was nearly destroyed by fire on August 5, 1930. The blaze began in the post office and spread to lumber along the railroad track. On November 10, 1952, it survived another major fire in which a child was killed.

Today Gore remains a small village off U.S. 50 west of Winchester with a post office, bank, fire company, a couple of churches, and several retail businesses. The area is sparsely populated compared to eastern and southern Frederick County. In 1985, an estimated 1,147 people lived at Gore, North Mountain Estates, and the surrounding countryside bounded by West Virginia, Great North Mountain and State Routes 703 and 752.

The community of Gore is named for Sidney Sophia Cather Gore, who is remembered as a teacher, a friend of the poor, and a widow who raised three successful sons. A page one story about her death that ran in the Winchester Evening Star *described her as "one of the best known and best beloved women in this part of the state." The daughter of James Cather and Nancy Howard, Gore was born in 1828 at Flint Ridge near Hayfield and died in 1906. Her brother was William Cather, the grandfather of novelist Willa Cather.*

first lived at Timber Ridge but moved to Back Creek, where their house burned, and, from there, moved to Valley Inn at Gore, which later was called Valley Home. Her husband operated a store and left her in debt when he died in 1861. To support her family, she got a job teaching school for $125 a year. She also earned money by offering food and lodging at Valley Home. A devout Baptist, Gore educated about thirty young men for the ministry and gave money to build the parsonage at Hebron Baptist Church.

Her three sons received college educations, with two becoming college professors and chairmen of math departments at their schools: Joshua W. Gore at the University of North Carolina at Chapel Hill and James Howard Gore at what is now George Washington University. Her son Perry Gore was sheriff of Frederick County. Courtesy of the Handley Library Archives

Pulitzer Prize-winning novelist Willa Cather as a child. She was born in 1873 at Gore, which was then called Back Creek Valley. Her birthplace, the home of her maternal grandmother, Rachel Seibert Boak, and Willow Shade, the brick house where her family moved the year after she was born, still stand on U.S. 50 west of Winchester and are designated by highway markers.

The Cathers lived at Willow Shade until they moved to Nebraska when Willa was nine. Some relatives suffered from tuberculosis and Willa's grandfather, William Cather, and other family members had already moved west in search of a drier climate. When the sheep barn at Willow Shade burned, Willa's father, Charles, joined them.

Cather wrote twelve novels in addition to poetry, short stories, and newspaper and magazine articles. She became a journalist after graduating from Lincoln State University and later was the editor of *McClure's* magazine. She received the Pulitzer Prize in 1923 for *One of Ours*, a story of a prairie boy in World War I. Two of her best-known novels about the prairie settlers are *O Pioneers* and *My Antonia*. Her final novel, *Sapphira and the Slave Girl*, is the only one

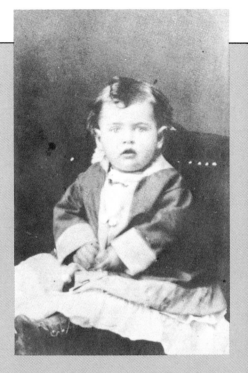

that is set in the Back Creek Valley. The mill in the book was based on one that stood along Back Creek and belonged to Rachel Boak's father, and some of the stories in the novel were based on those Cather had heard from her grandmother. Cather died in 1947. Carte de Visite by Wortham & Bowley of Winchester, courtesy of the Nebraska State Historical Society

James Howard Gore was a founder and life trustee of the National Geographic Society. The son of Sidney and Mahlon Gore, he was born in Gore in 1856. A world traveler, he was chairman of the math department at Columbia College, which now is George Washington University. He was a U.S. delegate to six international congresses and served on the board of directors of Dupont Bank and the National Library for the Blind. On January 13, 1888, he and thirty-three other men formed the National Geographic Society. Gore also was the author of books on geology, geodetics and mathematics and published a book about Sidney Gore, My Mother's Story, in 1920. Courtesy of the Handley Library Archives

Willow Shade was Willa Cather's childhood home from 1874 to 1883, when her family moved to Nebraska. It was built by her grandfather, William Cather, in 1858 and was the setting for the final chapters of her 1940 novel, Sapphira and the Slave Girl. The home is shown here as it appeared before U.S. 50 was built at the front of the property. It is one mile east of where she was born. Courtesy of the Nebraska State Historical Society

Charles Cather, author Willa Cather's father, was persuaded to join other family members in Nebraska after this sheep barn at Willow Shade burned in 1882. Willa did not want to go. This is how Mildred R. Bennett, editor of the Willa Cather Pioneer Memorial Newsletter in Red Cloud, Nebraska, described the Cathers's departure from Frederick County in a 1981 issue:

"As they started to drive away, across the fields came the loyal old sheep dog, barking and dragging her chain. Father could not stop Willa from jumping out of the carriage and running to the dog, hugging her and crying. Father had to pull her away and carry her to the carriage while someone else held the dog.

"And so Willa Cather left Virginia." Courtesy of the Nebraska Historical Society

Now the site of a Boy Scout camp, the Rock Enon Springs Hotel in the late 1900s was a flourishing late-nineteenth-century resort near Gore on State Route 683. No longer standing, the 450-room hotel provided elegant lodgings for guests who came by stagecoach to enjoy nearby mineral springs. Congressmen brought their families from Washington to spend the summers there. The original section of the hotel was built in 1856. An addition was torn down after 1919 and the remaining portion of the hotel was razed in 1942.

The property was earlier called Capper Springs for John Capper, a settler who built a cabin near the site of the future resort. The property changed hands several times before William Marker built the original section of the hotel. Marker established a post office in 1859, with himself as postmaster, and became partners with Mahlon Gore, the husband of Sidney Gore. Others owned the hotel after Marker, including the Rock Enon Springs Company, which increased the size of the original hotel to 450 rooms and built a large ballroom, a billiard room, a band pavilion, and an observation tower. Adam Pratt bought it in 1875 and added more land. He sold it to Fred Glaize and Lee Herrell in 1919, and Glaize sold the 570-acre site to the Shenandoah Area Council of the Boy Scouts of America in 1945. Courtesy of the Winchester-Frederick County Historical Society

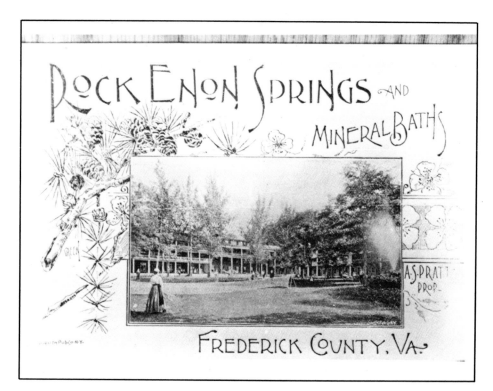

Men of the Hebron Baptist Church at Gore were photographed in 1910. Courtesy of the Winchester-Frederick County Historical Society

These undated photographs show the baseball team at Gore School and students at the school standing at attention as their classmates raise the flag. Gore and Gainesboro elementary schools were closed and replaced by Indian Hollow Elementary School in 1988. Courtesy of the Frederick County School Board Office

Back Creek native and historian Ralph Lee Triplett taught school for thirty-four years, mostly in Frederick County. He was born in 1898 and is shown below in a photograph taken in the early 1980s. Triplett wrote A History of Upper Back Creek, a collection of memories and oral history about the Gore area, which he described as a nineteenth-century timber paradise. He died at age eighty-six in 1984. Photo courtesy of Rual P. Anderson

Rual P. Anderson (above right) at his home near Gore. He was born in 1902 at nearby Maple Springs Farm and has lived in the Gore area all his life. A state forestry warden for thirty years, he was a member of the board of directors of Ebenezer Christian Church and Southern States and is currently chairman of the church's board of trustees. He is the author of a history book about the Gore area and two genealogies of local families, including one on the Spaids, Andersons, and Whitacres. Courtesy of Rual P. Anderson

As a youngster, Charles Parish, Jr., bore a strong resemblance to his father, Charles Parish, Sr. Both men are eight years old in these photographs, with the younger Parish on the left in 1927 and his father on the right in 1871. The older Parish was a farmer and orchardist who lived at Gore. He was born in 1863 and died in 1941. His son was born in 1919 and was the postmaster of Gore from 1949 until his death in 1969. Courtesy of Grace Parish, the wife of Charles Parish, Jr.

Star Tannery

Star Tannery, originally called Gravel Springs, is a community in southwestern Frederick County's Cedar Creek Valley. Nestled between the foothills of Big North Mountain on the west and Little North Mountain near the Shenandoah County line on the east, the community has long outlived the nineteenth-century tannery for which it was named.

In the 1800s the Star Shoe Company of Baltimore, Maryland, located a tannery at the settlement. Hides were tanned and sent elsewhere to be turned into shoes. Bark from the area's plentiful supply of oak and chestnut trees were used to tan the hides. The tannery provided jobs and the community prospered until near the end of the century, when the bark was used up and the tannery closed, about 1895.

Thomas Cover, who had bought the tannery from Star Shoe Company in 1868, established the annual Gravel Springs picnic. What began as a summer event for tannery employees has continued as an annual community celebration that is held next to Gravel Springs Lutheran Church on State Route 600. It is held the second Saturday in August because, according to Cover's calculations, it rarely rains on that date.

The small schoolhouses in the area were closed long ago but other institutions that bind the community have prospered. Today Star Tannery has a fire department and a post office. While most other areas of Frederick County got telephone service in the early twentieth century, Chesapeake & Potomac, which operates in the rest of Frederick County, did not extend to Star Tannery. The area was without telephone service until about 1960, when Shenandoah Telephone Company offered service to the community.

The estimated population in the Star Tannery area was 527 in 1985. Much of the area is part of the George Washington National Forest.

The Rev. William Jacob Smith was pastor of Gravel Springs Lutheran Church from 1885 until his death in 1911. Besides holding services at Gravel Springs, Reverend Smith also traveled four hundred miles a month to hold services at Bethel, St. John's, St. James, and Fremont Lutheran churches. His obituary in the Winchester Evening Star said Smith was a highly regarded minister who rarely missed an appointment and "turned a deaf ear to none." Smith was born in Boonesboro, Maryland, in 1845 and was a Union veteran. He graduated from Roanoke College and the Southern Theological Seminary, both in Salem, Virginia. Before coming to Gravel Springs, he was a pastor in Salisbury, North Carolina, and Roanoke. Reverend Smith also was a president of the Virginia Synod. He is buried at Mount Hebron Cemetery. Courtesy of Lt. Col. (Ret.) Fietta Rosenberger, his granddaughter

These men worked at the tannery that gave Star Tannery its name. They took a moment from their annual company picnic to pose for this undated photograph in front of Gravel Springs Luthern Church. Tannery owner Thomas Cover is the second man on the right in the second row from the bottom. He is standing with a hat in his right hand. Others identified in the photograph are, front row, starting at third from the left, Romanas Heishman, Charlie Rosenberger, George Tom Orndorff, Charlie Rudolph, Jim Renner, and Sam Himelright. Second row, from left, are William Henry Garrett, Dr. George H. Snarr, and, sixth from left, Ike McIlwee. Third row are, from left, Robert Himelright, seventh from left, Luther Himelright, and, eighth from left, Will Beeler. Back row, from left, Hunter Brill and Cover Himelright. Courtesy of David Brill

Abraham Brill was a farmer in Star Tannery. He was born in 1804 and died in 1884. Courtesy of his granddaughter, Elaine W. Hall

Grace and Ernest Cooper of Star Tannery are shown circa 1918 going for a spin in their Saxon automobile. Courtesy of Esther Cooper Moore, their daughter

The Cooper family of Star Tannery in 1922 are from left, Harold Cooper, Helen Dorner, Louisa Virginia Townes Cooper, John Henry Adams Cooper, Elsie Dorner, Ernest Cooper, and Esther Cooper. Courtesy of Esther Cooper Moore

Members of the Gravel Springs Band in 1910 are from left to right, front row: Allen Stine, Riley Godlove, Chain Askridge, Roy Heishman, and Arthur Orndorff; back row: Elijah Pifer, Jesse Stine, Albert Stine, S. R. Heishman, Hessler Himelright, Fred Heishman, and Cover Himelright. Courtesy of David Brill

Students at the Gravel Springs School at Star Tannery in an undated photograph. The woman at the left is teacher Hanna Funkhouser. Courtesy of David Brill

Many of the Whitacres in northwestern Frederick County trace their roots to Joshua Whitacre (1766-1814) and his ancestors. He settled along the banks of Isaac Creek about 1800 on land that is now The Summit, and was the first in his family to spell his name Whitacre instead of Whitaker. The eldest son of George Whitaker I, Joshua married Rachel Wilson and was the father of George Whitacre II and the grandfather of Nimrod Whitacre. Joshua's grandparents, John Whitaker II and Naiomi Hulme Whitaker, were married in Philadelphia in 1734 and later moved to New Jersey. Courtesy of Rual P. Anderson

This photograph was taken about 1891 at the George Kerns homeplace, near Ebenezer Christian Church. From left to right, front row: Rebecca Ann Kerns Whitacre; Ollie May Whitacre (little girl standing); Catherine Kerns Mellon; and Dow Sine Whitacre (boy standing); unidentified girl seated on the floor; George Kerns (man seated in center); Mary Kerns Parish, holding Pauline Arabell Parish; Mary Ellen Kerns Parish (seated on floor); Devlin Gordon Parish (standing behind Mary Ellen Kerns Parish); and Margaret E. Slonaker Parish (in chair on far right). Back row: Aglon Whitacre, Martha Kerns Fletcher, John W. Parish, George W. Parish, Charley W. Parish, and Franklin Perry Kerns. Courtesy of Rual P. Anderson

John Harrison Perry (1874-1951) lived on a farm at Mount Pleasant on State Route 608 with his wife, Mable Allemong Perry, and their eight children. He also had a sawmill and cut timber that was used for railroad cross ties. This photograph was taken about 1900. Courtesy of his daughter, Bessie Williams

Students at the Friendly Grove School in 1902. The school closed in 1934, and the building is now a community center at the entrance to a community park at Mountain Falls. From left to right, front row: Frances Bucher Tevault, Clara Clowser Kline, Annie Orndorff, a girl whose last name is Marker, Genetta Smith Rosenberger, a girl whose last name is Rupell, Frisbie Smith, Carrol "Bud" Clowser, and Edwin Smith. Second row: Dave Williams, Cleta Clowser, Staton Cooper, Rena Clowser, Mae Clowser, Mary Tevault, Clifton Cave, Vernie Tevault, and Cleve Bucher. Back row: Jack Bucher, Mrs. Rupell, Jim Bucher, and Pat Williams. Courtesy of William F. Triplett

Whether for sport or out of necessity, deer hunting has long been popular in Frederick County. This buck was killed on North Mountain in 1910. The hunters are from Hayfield. From left to right, front row: Oscar Kline, Boyd Presley Ramey, and Stan Bayliss. Back row: Conley Bayliss. The man with the gun pointed at the deer is unidentified. Courtesy of Ramey's grandson, Boyd P. Ramey

This photograph of the Roanoke School near Mt. Williams was taken in April 1914 by Frances B. Larrick Adams, who taught at the school between 1907 and 1910 and whose photograph appears in this book. The building, which was on the Newtown Road (now an unmaintained extension of State Route 612) is no longer standing. Courtesy of Lewis A. Williams

The Rev. H. E. H. Sloop (seated) and his family are shown in this 1918 photograph. He was the minister of St. John's Lutheran Church in Mt. Williams and the Gravel Springs and St. James Lutheran churches of Star Tannery. Courtesy of Lewis A. Williams

Lydia Ann Plum and her husband, Abraham Vance Plum, in 1917 in front of their log home at Pembroke Springs in Mountain Falls. The photograph was taken by their grandson, William Cecil Hodgson, while he was on leave from the Army during World War I. Plum was a first corporal in Company D of the Thirty-third Virginia Regiment during the Civil War. He was born in 1842, married right after the war, and had a blacksmith shop at Gore. He died in 1928. Lydia Plum was born in 1837 and died in 1923. Courtesy of their great-grandson, William F. Triplett

115

This is the wedding picture of Hurl and Ima Himelright, who were married March 28, 1918 and lived at Mt. Williams. Hurl Himelright, a Republican, was the Back Creek representative to the Frederick County Board of Supervisors in the 1950s. He was born in 1895 and turned ninety-two in 1987. Ima Himelright was born in 1898 and died in 1987. Courtesy of their nephew, Lewis A. Williams

These children were students at Lamp's School about 1930 to 1933. This public school, on State Route 608, was located in the Back Creek District. It closed in 1934. Courtesy of the Winchester-Frederick County Historical Society

The Mt. Williams Store on State Route 608 in 1957. Photo by J. A. Seals; courtesy of the Winchester-Frederick County Historical Society

Assistant Chief Steve Smith (left) and Chief Marion Clowser of the North Mountain Fire Company stand on either side of a 1986 Ford four-wheel-drive attack unit. Photo by Alan Lehman of the Northern Virginia Daily; courtesy of Marion Clowser

Gainesboro

The village of Gainesboro on U.S. 522 north of Winchester was originally named Pughtown for the family that settled the area in the eighteenth century and their son who laid out its first lots.

Quakers Jesse Pugh, Sr., and his wife, Alice, came to Frederick County from Philadelphia, Pennsylvania, to Hopewell Meeting in Clearbrook on July 28, 1741. Pugh obtained a large tract of land on both sides of Back Creek from Lord Fairfax on January 2, 1753, and sold 260 acres to his son, Job, in 1793. The younger Pugh made a plat of the land in 1797 and drafted a charter for Pughtown on October 6, 1788. Trustees of the town were George Ruble, who leased ten acres from Jesse Pugh, Sr., for a mill and other buildings, and Job's brother, Jesse Pugh, Jr. Streets, building restrictions, and fees were established and rent for each lot was set at one dollar a year. On April 28, 1806, Job sold his brother Jesse the village of Pughtown with the exception of a Quaker meetinghouse that is no longer standing. The church's graveyard remains on a hill across from the village. Jesse sold the land to Joseph Gordon in 1808, who passed it on to his son, John.

After 1820, the deeds refer to the town as Gainesboro. When Frederick County was divided into districts in 1870, Gainesboro became the name of a district, with Pughtown as the name of one of its precincts.

In 1985, the population of the Gainesboro area, including Whitacre, Cross Junction, and The Summit, was estimated at 1,672.

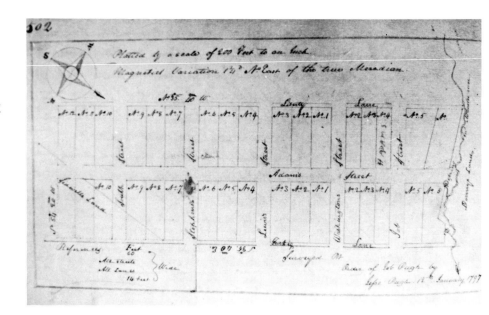

The village of Gainesboro originally was named Pughtown. This plat was recorded in the Frederick County Circuit Court clerk's office on January 12, 1797. Photo by Irv Lavitz

Marcus H. Larrick and his wife, Augusta Bean Larrick, and their daughters are seen here in 1897. The photograph was taken while they were in Washington, D.C., for the innauguration of William B. McKinley. The daughter standing just behind her parents is Pearl Larrick; Mary Larrick Adams is the smaller girl standing between her parents; Grace Larrick Emmart is seated at left, and Frances Larrick Adams is seated at the right. They lived at Meadow View on Indian Hollow Road near Hayfield. Marcus Larrick was born in 1855 and married Augusta Larrick on Christmas Day 1877. Augusta Larrick was born in 185 and died in 1930. Pearl was born in 1879; Mary was born in 1887; Grace was born in 1881; and Frances was born in 1885. Courte of Frances Adams Unger, the daughter of M Larrick Adams

This building, photographed about 1910, once held White's Fort near Hayfield, west of Hogue Creek. It burned about 1919 and consisted of two structures four feet apart joined by wood. The older structure, built about 1732, was the home of Dr. Robert White, one of Frederick County's first settlers and physicians. Born in Scotland, he was a captain and surgeon in the British navy before he immigrated to the colonies. The fort, the taller structure in the photograph, and a stockade were built by his son, Maj. Robert White, in 1763. It was a private fort to protect White's family and neighbors at Great North Mountain from Indians. In July 1763, White heard that Indians were along the Great Cacapon River and warned his neighbors to come to the fort. Owen Thomas, a farmer who wouldn't leave his harvest, was killed by Indians. White again learned that Indians were nearby in June 1764 and warned his neighbors to take cover at the fort. More than twenty people took his advice but were attacked along the way by Delaware Indians. Most were killed. Some were captured but escaped. One woman who was scalped survived. Courtesy of Grace and Merle Moore

James Bean, Jr., was born in 1810 and died in 1875. He was the son of Maj. James Bean, Sr., who built Taylor Furnace at North Mountain, and the grandson of pioneer settler Mordecai Bean. James Jr. married Gulielma Fawcett in 1839. They had seven children. Courtesy of Frances Adams Unger

119

Classes were once held at Cross Roads School west of Winchester near the intersection of state routes 600 and 679. Indian Hollow Elementary School, which replaced Gore and Gainesboro elementary schools, is on State Route 600, near the site of this old one-room school. Students in this photograph are shown on the last day of a school term circa 1909. The school closed in 1934. Those identified in the line nearest the camera, from left, are Russell Ramey; third from left, Julian A. Larrick; Bessie Jackson DeHaven; Leslie H. Ramey; Beulah Rosenberger Grove; Stephen Whitacre; Madeline Anderson Holland; Harriet Anderson Pingley; Roy Rinker; and Julian Rosenberger. Among the people in the background are Lloyd Rosenberger, Mary Larrick Adams, Mable Jackson Hawkins, Grace Larrick Emmart, Ray Anderson, Angie Larrick Richard, Lena Larrick Orndorff, Orrah Bayliss Reid, Charley Reid, and Robert Rinker. The teacher at the school was Beulah Rogers Luttrell. Courtesy of Sharon Grove Kelley

The Redland School in Whitacre in 1912. Originally a one-room schoolhouse, a second room was added in 1916. It closed in 1936. Known today as the Whitacre Community Building, the structure is owned by the Redland Methodist Church. Courtesy of Hilda Lizer

The Hayfield Fishing Club on an outing at the Cacapon River in 1914. Courtesy of Grace and Merle Moore

Ida Bell Thwaite posed with her daughters and her son's wife in 1924 at her home in Albin on U.S. 522. From left are Ida Thwaite, daughter Louise Thwaite Solenberger, daughter-in-law Onedia Thwaite, and daughter Nina Thwaite Schlack. Courtesy of Mary Lou Koontz, Nina Schlack's daughter

Vernon and Frances Adams Unger of Albin were married December 7, 1940. This photograph was taken just before Vernon Unger left for the Army in 1943. He was in the service for nearly three years, training at Ft. Eustis in Little Rock, Arkansas, and was stationed in England, France, and Germany. Courtesy of Frances Adams Unger

Lamarian and Jacob Rinker were the first residents of an old house near Sunnyside that was once known as Braddock Heights Farm and whose address is now 1101 Fox Drive. Jacob Rinker built the house between 1785 and 1804 on land that he got from his father, Casper, a Swiss immigrant. Their last name was originally Ringger. Lamarian was born in 1770. Jacob was born in 1764 and died in 1837. About 1831 they sold the house to William and Mary Von Fahnestock; it is now owned by the Von Fahnestocks's great-grandson, Burrell C. Luttrell. Courtesy of Evelyn Bywaters Goode, a Rinker descendant

Josiah Fries and his wife, Margaret Ellen Boyd Fries, lived near the Quaker Cemetery on Apple Pie Ridge. They were married on March 27, 1843, and had seven children and a foster daughter. Their photographs are dated about 1892. Fries was born in 1821 and died in 1901. He was a farmer, a veterinary surgeon, and a member of the United Brethren Church. His grandfather, German immigrant Martin Fries, came to Frederick County in 1789 after living in York, Pennsylvania. Margaret Fries was born in 1826 and died in 1894. Photos by Davidson Brothers at the Masonic Temple in Winchester, courtesy of Lucille Y. Sencindiver

Mable Kathryn Haynes Bond, Frederick County's second home extension agent, was about six years old in this 1899 photograph. She is sitting on the knee of her grandmother, Mary Ann Hayes Maxwell. Born in Charlton, New York, in 1893, Mable Haynes took her job as the county's extension agent in 1918 and resigned in 1920 after she married Allen Bond of Apple Pie Ridge. Courtesy of Catherine P. Anderson

David and Rachel Hott and their family lived just north of Whitehall. This photograph was taken about 1900. From left to right, front row: Laura Izola Hott Dailey, David Fries Hott, Rachel Hancher Hott, and David Hott. Back row: Franklin Hott, Frannie Bell Hott Sencindiver, John Hott, Lucie Ellen Hott Kiver, Annie Hott Randall, Aria Anna Hott Flagg, and Emma Tanquary Hott Anderson. Courtesy of Lucille Y. Sencindiver

Dorothy Flowers was a third grade teacher at the Welltown School, on State Route 672, west of Welltown Pike. The school closed in 1936. Courtesy of Mary Ebert

Arch McCarroll and his wife, Virginia Manuel Moulden McCarroll, in their wedding picture. Virginia McCarroll ran a dance hall in Brucetown in the 1930s. Arch McCarroll was a farmer and a construction worker who helped to build Handley High School. Courtesy of Pearl Lake Ebert

Students of the Whitehall Graded School were in Winchester on April 24, 1914, for the first annual school fair. More than two thousand pupils from the city and Frederick County marched in a parade downtown, and there were more than six hundred exhibits of students' work displayed at John Kerr School at Cameron and Cork streets. A newspaper account said the event drew more people to Winchester than any other occasion except for Confederate Memorial Day. Teacher Ida Taylor Gordon is at the far right and the uniformed man behind her is bus driver U. S. Fries. The children in the photograph are not identified, but are members of prominent families from Whitehall, Apple Pie Ridge, Grimes, Green Spring, and Cedar Grove. Among them are Andersons, Browns, Dicks, Lodges, Shepards, Smiths, and Strothers. The horse-drawn bus, decorated with flags, is an example of the county's first school buses. There was no glass in the windows and students had to unfurl the bus's canvas weather beaters when it started to rain. Courtesy of James V. Hutton, Jr.

Students at the Brucetown School on March 29, 1909. On the far right is their teacher, Belle C. Jobe. The school closed in 1941. Courtesy of the Handley Library Archives

William H. Lawrence, Jr., and his original thirteen employees posed for this picture shortly after he bought the Clearbrook Woolen Mill on April 13, 1939. From left to right are: front row, Wesley Brill, boilerman; Gavin "Scotty" Binner, dyer (later superintendent); Jack Willis, assistant dryer; Ray Russell, loom fixer; Hugh T. "Bud" Brill, carder; and Lawrence. In the back row are June Scrivener Aikins, secretary; Woodrow Puffinberger, boss weaver; Bill Swartz, warp dresser; Lester Keckley, mechanic; Ted Eckman, finisher; Harry McAboy, master mechanic; Albert Clark, boss carder; and Hubert Kelchner, boss spinner. The mill was a successor of the Brucetown Woolen Mill, two miles to the east, which had burned in the early 1930s. The mill made mostly fancy women's wear and tweeds, but during World War II it made one thousand olive-drab army blankets a day, operating three shifts, six days a week. Some area soldiers were issued Clearbrook woolen blankets during the war. The mill closed in 1971, and the site was occupied by Seaward International, a manufacturer of marine equipment. A lake and recreation park for employees also was sold to Frederick County and became Clearbrook Park. The Clearbrook Woolen Shop, which sells blankets and fabric, still operates today on U.S. 11. Courtesy of William H. Lawrence, Jr.

Over the years Kenilworth on U.S. 11 north of Winchester has been a nursing home, the site of a Union general's party near the end of the Civil War, and the home of a millionaire playboy who murdered a famous architect. William Stephenson, for whom the nearby community is named, bought the property in 1823 and called it Kenilworth after his family home in Ireland. Part of the original estate became the Frederick County Fairgrounds.

John Littler first owned the property. He received a 1,332-acre grant from the governor of Virginia in 1735 and is believed to have built the section of the house that today is the garage and upstairs apartment. His grandsons later built the main part of the house in stages between 1742 and 1800. Littler called his home Rocktown and operated a tavern there. He married Mary Ross of nearby Waverly Farm.

The heirs of Elijah Littler sold the house to William Stephenson, and it remained in his family for almost a century. During the Civil War it was a headquarters of Confederate Gen. Jubal Early and later for Union

Brevet-Major Gen. William H. Emory, who threw a party there near the end of the war that was reported in the New York Times.

Harry K. Thaw bought the house in 1924 as a quiet retreat from his stormy past. He made national news when he murdered Standford White, a famous architect. Thaw suspected White was having an affair with his wife, Evelyn Nesbit, a New York model, and shot the architect while he was watching a performance on the Madison Square Garden Roof in New York. Two sensational trials followed, with Thaw escaping prison when he was acquitted

on the grounds of insanity. Thaw's story was incorporated into E. L. Doctorow's best-selling novel Ragtime.

Dr. Charles R. Anderson, former mayor of Winchester, bought the home after Thaw's death and for years it housed Kenilworth Nursing Home. In 1973, Charles W. Orndoff, who owns a Whitehall abattoir and represents the Stonewall District on the Frederick County Board of Supervisors, bought the house at auction and sold part of the property to the Frederick County Fair Association. Photo by Teresa Lazazzera

Emmanuel United Methodist Church at U.S. 11 and State Route 664 was built in 1887 on land near the old Stephenson train depot. The congregation's roots can be traced to Milburn Chapel, another Stephenson church that once stood on State Route 662 at the Harry McCann farm. It was damaged during the Civil War and never restored. Courtesy of J. Meredith Ashwood

The old Stephenson Post Office on State Route 664 near the old Stephenson's Depot before it closed in August 1981. The post office was replaced by a larger, modern facility on U.S. 11. Courtesy of the Winchester Star

Some members of John Wesley Community Christian Church at Cedar Hill pose after Sunday morning services in July 1987. Keydish Ford (left) holds her one-year-old nephew, Dante Jackson, son of Dezell and Carlisa Jackson, and James Dokes, Sr., holds his son, James, Jr. Cedar Hill is a black community in Clearbrook west of U.S. 11 on a dirt road off State Route 671. Peter Hamilton and Douglas Carter donated one and a half acres for the church in 1884, but the original building burned and the existing church was built about 1921. Before integration, the children of Cedar Hill attended a one-room schoolhouse at the entrance to the community. It is not known how Cedar Hill got its name, which is the same as abolitionist Frederick Douglass's home in Anacostia. Some say the name was for the cedars that once grew there and were cut to prevent a scale from spreading to nearby apple orchards. Photo by Rick Foster; courtesy of the Winchester Star

Once an elegant resort where the well-to-do enjoyed the medicinal benefits of the nearby white sulphur springs, and later a Catholic seminary, the old Jordan Springs Hotel is now the home of Shalom et Benedictus, a drug and alcohol treatment center.

The four-story, sixty-room hotel was built in 1893 by Claredon Jordan. The property was passed down through his family by his great-uncle, Branch Jordan, who bought it in the early 1800s and built the first hotel there. A second hotel was built in 1855, and Claredon's father, Edwin C. Jordan, inherited it when Branch Jordan died in 1861. During the Civil War, it was used as a hospital by both the Northern and Southern armies.

Claredon Jordan inherited the property when his father died in 1890, but business dropped off after a newspaper reported an outbreak of typhoid at the hotel. The resort was sold to Henry H. Baker in 1905 and closed in 1916. Several attempts to revive the old hotel failed. It was used briefly in the early 1950s by the Franklin Foundation of Philadelphia as an anticommunist school. The Most Holy Trinity, a Catholic missionary community, used the hotel as a seminary for training priests from 1954 to 1972. The Trinitarians allowed Shalom to use the building beginning in 1972 and then donated it to Shalom in 1984. Courtesy of the Winchester Star

The old Jordan Spring Hotel east of U.S. 11 on State Route 664 was once a posh and popular nineteenth-century resort. As this advertisement promised, visitors were met by a carriage at Stephenson's Depot and driven to the hotel in style. Courtesy of the Winchester Star

JORDAN'S
WHITE
SULPHUR SPRINGS,

FREDERICK COUNTY, VIRGINIA.

Will be OPEN for the RECEPTION of VISITORS on the 16th of JUNE, 1856.

Since last season the Buildings have undergone thorough repair, painting, &c.

These SPRINGS are situated in one of the most healthy and beautiful portions of Virginia, one and a half miles from STEPHENSON'S DEPOT, a point on the Harper's Ferry and Winchester Rail Road, five miles from Winchester.

PASSENGERS *leaving WASHINGTON, BALTIMORE or CUMBERLAND* by the early MORNING TRAIN, arrive at the SPRINGS the same day, in time to dine.

From WELDON, N.C., via NORFOLK, VA., in the Evening, by the Steamers LOUISIANA or NORTH CAROLINA, arrive in BALTIMORE in full time to connect with the Morning Train to Harper's Ferry and the Springs. *From STAUNTON, VA.* on the Afternoon of the same day. *From PETERSBURG or RICHMOND* in the Evening, arrive in Washington next Morning in due time to take the Early Train to the Springs.

To those in pursuit of Health or Pleasure, this is a pleasant resort during the Summer months. In Dyspepsia, Diseases of the Liver and Spleen, Chronic affections of the Brain, Nervous Complaints, Rheumatism, Gout, the various forms of Dropsy, Mercurial Diseases, and *especially* in Eruptive diseases, its Curative Medicinal Qualities are well known and fully established.

RICE'S Celebrated BALTIMORE COTILLION BAND, and EXPERIENCED SERVANTS,
Are Engaged for the Season

MAILS DAILY, EXCEPT SUNDAY.

COACHES await the Arrival of the Cars at STEPHENSON'S DEPOT to Convey PASSENGERS to the SPRINGS

E. C. & R. M. JORDAN & BRO.,
PROPRIETORS.

Address JORDAN'S W. S. SPRINGS, Frederick Co., Va.

Apples
and
Agriculture

This apple tree on Apple Pie Ridge was among the first planted in Frederick County. It was part of a five-acre orchard of Smith Cider apples planted by a Hessian prisoner during the Revolutionary War. From left to right are Mary Maxwell Bond, Barbara Bond, Allen Bond, and Nancy Bond. Courtesy of Catherine P. Anderson

Apples

Virginia was the sixth largest apple producer in the country in 1986, and about 40 percent of the state's crop comes from orchards in Frederick County.

The apple industry is most visible during May blossoming and the fall harvest, which begins around Labor Day, but raising apples is actually a year-round job. Trees are pruned during the first few months of the year and then sprayed for disease and insects in April and July.

Among the varieties grown locally are Red Delicious, Golden Delicious, Jonathans, Grimes Golden, Stayman, Yorks, Rambos, and Greening. They are sent to processing firms in Virginia, Pennsylvania, and New York and end up on grocers's shelves or in products such as cider, vinegar, juice, applesauce, apple rings, apple butter, and apple pies. Among the largest local buyers are National Fruit Products Company, Inc., and Zeropack in Winchester, Knouse Foods Cooperative, Inc., in Pennsylvania, and Bowman Apple Products Company in Mt. Jackson.

Controlled atmosphere facilities have lengthened the amount of time that apples can be stored. The largest controlled atmosphere storage facilities in the region, Winchester Cold Storage and the Virginia Apple Storage Company, are in Winchester. For regular storage, apples are cooled to about thirty degrees and can be kept until spring. In controlled atmosphere, apples are chilled and placed in a sealed storage facility, where the amount of oxygen is reduced to stop apples from ripening.

Frederick County orchardists have come to rely less on the local labor force in recent years and more on migrant workers to pick their apples. At the Frederick County Labor Camp in 1985 there were about two hundred domestic pickers and eight hundred Jamaican workers.

Origins of Frederick County's Apple Industry

The presence of apples in Frederick County dates back to the eighteenth century, when a Hessian prisoner planted trees on Apple Pie Ridge during the Revolutionary War. Dr. George Stephens, a great grandson of pioneer Peter Stephens, planted trees in his orchard near Stephens City. Originally called Newtown Pippins, the apples became famous as Albemarle Pippins when Stephens moved to Albemarle County.

Dr. John S. Lupton was a leader among local nineteenth-century apple pioneers, and Thomas Wood Steck became one of the state's leading apple growers in the early twentieth century. They were followed by Harry F. Byrd, Sr., who became one of the largest apple

Apples trees were sold in eighteenth-century Frederick County as shown by this newspaper advertisement, which ran in 1790 in the Virginia Centinel or the Winchester Mercury. Courtesy of the Handley Library Archives

growers in the world. Lupton's twenty acres of Newtown Pippins on Northwestern Grade made up the first commercial apple orchard west of the Blue Ridge Mountains. Steck raised prize-winning apples in his orchards in the Opequon District. He was one of the first to realize the potential of orchards in this area.

Origins of the Shenandoah Apple Blossom Festival

The Shenandoah Apple Blossom Festival began as a one-day event in 1924 with a proclamation by Mayor William W. Glass, Sr., a few decorated cars, and the coronation of Elizabeth Steck as the first Queen Shenandoah on the steps of the old George Washington Hotel.

The festival drew more than thirty thousand people its first year. The Grand Feature Parade lasted forty-five minutes and the grand marshal was Lewis M. Allen, a local physician and horse breeder.

The announcement of the first festival came at the organizational meeting of the Shenandoah Valley, Inc., a regional chamber of commerce formed in January 1924 to boost tourism and economic development. It is now called the Shenandoah Valley Travel Association.

"We Want the WORLD to Know Best Apples Grow in Shenandoah," the cover of the festival's 1924 program book declared. In it Harry F. Byrd, Sr., said the festival ought to become an annual event. "It would be an effective method of bringing the public to unconsciously associate apples with the Valley of Virginia," he wrote.

In the years that followed, the festival grew along with the apple industry. On April 20, 1930, the *New*

York Times, citing the seventh festival, listed Winchester as one of the ten most interesting places in the world. Today the festival is a four-day extravaganza with an annual budget of three hundred thousand dollars. Crowds estimated at 250,000 flood Winchester on the day of the Grand Feature Parade. Over the years, parade grand marshals have included entertainers such as Bob Hope, Ed Sullivan, Bing Crosby, Lucille Ball, and Robert Wagner. Television stars, such as Hal Linden, and politicians, such as Presidents Lyndon B. Johnson and Gerald R. Ford and Virginia Gov. Charles S. Robb, have also come to Winchester for their daughters's coronations as festival queens.

Isaac H. Moore is standing at the top of this apple train in the late 1910s. A steam engine was used to transport barrels of apples from the orchard. Courtesy of Grace Moore and Merle Moore, son of Isaac H. Moore

---

Frequency County Apple Crop

Frederick County Apple Crop	
1910....	351,490 bushels (smallest on record)
1920....	1,019,546 bushels
1925....	1,280,000 bushels
1930....	2,125,000 bushels
1935....	1,688,000 bushels
1940....	2,034,000 bushels
1945....	2,479,000 bushels
1950....	1,627,000 bushels
1954....	3,592,000 bushels
1960....	2,500,000 bushels
1966....	1,189,000 bushels
1970....	3,420,000 bushels
1976....	2,650,000 bushels
1982....	4,710,000 bushels (largest on record)
1986....	4,425,000 bushels

Sources: U.S. Census, Virginia Crop Reports, and the Virginia Agricultural Statistics Service

Agriculture

Frederick County was Virginia's leading wheat producer in the nineteenth century. In this century, apples have been the leading local crop. Other major early twentieth-century local crops included corn, wheat, potatoes, oats, hay, buckwheat, rye, peaches, and other fruit, according to the U.S. Census and Virginia Crop Reports from 1910 to 1928. Cattle, hogs, sheep, and chickens also were raised. There were dairies and egg factories. Farmers also produced food for themselves. "Every farm has its milk cows," according to *An Economic and Social Survey of Frederick County*, a 1930 report by the University of Virginia.

In 1925, there were 1,856 farms on 215,050 acres, about three-fourths of the land in Frederick County. About 3,712 people were employed in agriculture.

Agriculture continues to play an important role in the local economy even through there is less farm land and fewer people are employed in agriculture. While the amount of land in orchards has declined steadily in recent years, apple production has increased through the use of varieties that take up less acreage. The amount of land used for other farming purposes has fluctuated.

According to Virginia Employment Commission statistics, the number of people in Frederick County employed in agriculture has dwindled, with more people employed today in manufacturing, retail, and service areas. In March 1975, 877 people were employed in agriculture, about one-tenth of the county workforce. The number rose to 911 in March 1980. In March 1985, 294 people had agricultural jobs and 55 people had jobs in agricultural services out of a labor force of 8,984 people. These numbers do not include seasonal workers for orchards. The number of farms also has fallen from 1,500 in 1950 to 564 in 1974. Since then, however, the number of farms and land in farming has increased. In 1982, there were 632 farms on 126,087 acres, according to the U.S. Census Bureau.

Workers at Ed Grove's apple orchard on Middle Road proudly show off the fruits of their labor about 1913. Grove is seated near the center holding a branch of apples and his wife is standing to his left with apples in her hand. Apple pickers boarded at Grove's farm during the harvest. Courtesy of Paul and Garnette Beatty

The Grand Feature Parade of the second Shenandoah Apple Blossom Festival in 1925. The parade is on East Piccadilly Street headed west. The large apple on the float is an early version of the red cement apple in front of the Elks Lodge at Braddock and Piccadilly streets that has become a well-known Winchester landmark. The original apple was eight-by-six feet, hollow, and made of plaster of paris. Courtesy of the Winchester-Frederick County Historical Society

Winchester students performing in the 1939 Shenandoah Apple Blossom pageant on the steps of Handley High School. City Schools Superintendent Garland R. Quarles wrote and directed the pageant for nearly three decades beginning in 1931. It was part of the coronation ceremony for the festival queen. The ceremony has since been moved inside the school. Courtesy of Beverley Barr Hainer

Apples were once packed in barrels, such as these in 1926 at the Snapp family's orchard on Middle Road. Bertie Snapp is at the left grading apples while other workers pack them into barrels. Her son, Alfred Snapp, Sr., is standing on a platform at the far right. Ralph Snapp is standing left of the barrel at the center of the photograph. Courtesy of Alfred Snapp, Sr.

The Winchester Cold Storage on North Loudoun Street was said to be the largest cold storage for apples in the world after a 1929 addition was built. This postcard photograph was taken in the 1930s. Still operating today, the cold storage's claim as the largest is no longer true but remains on the front of the building. Between the Winchester plant, which holds 1.5 million bushels, and another in Charles Town, West Virginia, which holds about 735,000 bushels, Winchester Cold Storage holds about one percent of the apple crop in the United States.

The original building was constructed in 1917; the addition in 1923. It was built by a corporation headed by Harry F. Byrd, Sr., who had the largest apple orchards in the world. In 1961, the cold storage became the first in the Appalachian region to use controlled atmosphere storage. Today it continues to operate as a storage company for local growers and for processors. Courtesy of Margaret Rowe

Orchardist D. K. Russell, left, inspects apples with Russell Morrison, his foreman for more than fifty years. This photograph was one of several taken in 1949 for an article about Russell's success as an apple and peach orchardist that appeared in the April issue of Country Gentleman magazine. Photos from the article also were used in a Country Gentleman advertisement that ran in Newsweek magazine.

Russell was born in 1893, entered the apple business in 1919, and died in 1970. He lived on Welltown Pike, was the founder of D. K. Russell & Sons, and was president of the Frederick County Fruit Growers Association and the Winchester Apple Growers. Morrison was born in 1909 and died in 1983. Courtesy of J. Robert and Colleen Russell

J. Robert Russell of Apple Pie Ridge has collected more than seven hundred apple crates. Most are from local orchards but some are from as far away as Michigan and South Carolina. Crates replaced barrels as the standard method for storing apples in the early twentieth century, and crates were replaced by bins about 1960. Russell was born in 1919 and is the son of D. K. Russell. Today he and his brothers run the orchards their father started. Russell was the Gainesboro District representative to the Frederick County Board of Supervisors from 1968-1976 and its vice chairman his last four years in office. A charter member of the Stonewall Ruritan Club, he has had perfect attendance since 1951. Photo by Ray K. Saunders; courtesy of the Winchester Star

Jamaican and Puerto Rican apple pickers and orchard manager Aubrey M. Stickley (center) at Stewart Bell, Jr.'s orchard on Cedar Creek Grade on October 21, 1976. From the Stewart Bell Collection; courtesy of the Winchester-Frederick County Historical Society

Fred Knox and Cecil Cooper raking hay circa 1914 at the Cooper Farm in Star Tannery. Courtesy of Esther Cooper Moore

This is what a standard garden tractor looked like in 1934. Ernest T. Cooper is pictured at a farm in Star Tannery. Courtesy of Esther Cooper Moore

Brothers Dennis A. Cole and Lawrence P. Cole ran the Red Bud Dairy in the 1930s. This was a cap to one of the glass bottles they used. They delivered milk to homes and creameries. The business was on Red Bud Road near Va. 7. The dairy industry was important to early twentieth-century Frederick County. Courtesy of their niece, Linda Sutton

Farmers once used teams of horses to thresh wheat, as shown in this photograph taken about 1920 at Fawcett's Gap on Cedar Creek Grade. Julian Fawcett is driving the horses. Behind him on the thresher is his father, Clarkson Fawcett. His brother, Lewis Fawcett, is on the far right and farmhand William Orndorff is in the center. Courtesy of Julian's daughter, Lucy Fawcett Lamp

Workers pose with a steam engine used to thresh wheat on a farm at Star Tannery. Isaac H. Moore is second from the right with his hand on the engine. The others are unidentified. Courtesy of Grace and Merle Moore

The Sunnyside Dairy on Senseny Road was in business for more than sixty years. George P. Kern and his son, Roy, operated the dairy until 1947, delivering milk to Winchester seven days a week. For a while they offered the only home milk delivery in the city. They later signed a contract to deliver all their milk twice a day to Winchester Memorial Hospital in ten-gallon cans. Afterward, they sold milk to Haldeman Creamery, which then was at the Creamery Building on South Kent Street. The Kerns had the area's only herd of Golden Guernsey cows, whose milk brought high prices because of its high butterfat content. Courtesy of Roy Kern's wife, Esther L. Kern

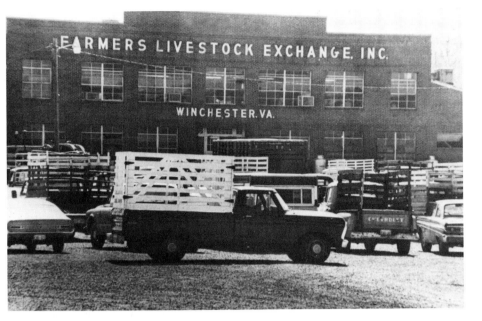

Cattle, hogs, and lambs are sold every Monday at the Farmers Livestock Exchange on U.S. 50 west of Winchester. Bidders sit in the grandstand as an auctioneer calls out prices. Livestock raised locally or brought from as far away as Pennsylvania, New York, and New Jersey circle the ring. Horses and goats are sometimes sold. A group of local farmers formed the exchange in the late 1940s and continues to own and operate it. The first sale was held October 10, 1947. Courtesy of the Winchester Star

9

Old and New

Dr. James A. Miller of Winchester sits among treasures of the area's medical history. On the left is a Union chest that was taken by Confederate troops early in the Civil War. On the right is one that dates back to colonial days. Miller, who was born in 1904, is the great-great grandson of German immigrant Godfrey Miller, who ran an eighteenth-century Winchester apothecary shop. His great-uncle, Godfrey Miller II, established Miller's Drug Store on Loudoun Street. Miller has written about the history of local medicine and says physicians were among the earliest settlers. He was named historian of the year by the Winchester-Frederick County Historical Society in 1988. Photo by Rick Foster; courtesy of the Winchester Star

In Frederick County and Winchester, as in other places, changes from old ways to new have affected every aspect of people's lives. Going to school, seeing a doctor, and working are very different activities today than they were just a few generations ago.

Medicine

The practice of medicine has a rich heritage in Winchester and Frederick County. Doctors, such as Scotch immigrant Robert White, were among the county's early pioneers. German immigrant Godfrey Miller, who came to Winchester in 1763, opened an apothecary shop at Leicester and Loudoun streets. His son, Godfrey Miller II, inherited the business and opened Miller's Drug Store at 107 North Loudoun Street in 1815. It remains in business today and is believed to be the oldest continually operated drugstore in the United States.

The first medical college in Virginia was in Winchester at Boscawen and Stewart streets. It was chartered in 1826 and was originally called the Medical School of the Valley of Virginia. It was opened by doctors John Esten Cooke and Hugh Holmes McGuire but was dormant by 1829, when two of its teachers left. It was revived in 1847 with a new name, Winchester Medical College. Classes were held until its students left at the outbreak of the Civil War.

The eagerness of its students for anatomical specimens may have inadvertently led to the school's demise. Students hopped a Winchester & Potomac train for Harpers Ferry, West Virginia, when they heard of John Brown's raid on the federal arsenal in 1859 and returned with a corpse that turned out to be the body of one of John Brown's sons. When Union forces entered Winchester in March 1862, the preserved body was sent north and the school was burned.

Winchester Memorial Hospital, the forerunner of Winchester Medical Center, opened in 1903. It was built for fifteen thousand dollars. Col. William Byrd, Mrs. Lewis Hyde of Berryville and New York, and merchant-philanthropist Charles B. Rouss donated five thousand dollars each. There was opposition to the new hospital and only twenty-five dollars for it was raised in Frederick County, where it was called a "slaughter house."

A petition to charter the hospital was filed on May 27, 1901. Dr. Hunter Holmes McGuire was named president of the corporation and ran the hospital until his death in the late 1940s. The ladies' auxiliary raised funds for a horse-drawn ambulance in 1905. It was replaced by a motor ambulance in 1920. The early hospital also had a training school for nurses, and local resident Mary Milliner was its first graduate in 1905. The nursing school was replaced in 1964, when Shenandoah College and Conservatory began its nursing program.

Over the years the hospital has struggled to keep up with the growth of Winchester and Frederick County. It is now a regional facility, with 28 percent of its patients coming from West Virginia, 16 to 20 percent coming from Warren and Shenandoah counties and a significant number from western Loudoun County.

An entrance on Stewart Street and an addition on Cork Street were built in 1927. The building on Stewart was replaced by the current five-story building in 1951. The towers on Cork Street opened in 1964, giving the hospital more patient rooms and its first psychiatric unit. Two more floors were added in 1976, and the McGuire wing, which houses the emergency room, was built in 1979.

For years, residents surrounding the hospital have complained about lack of parking. Old houses in the neighborhood had to be torn down to make room for hospital expansion and parking lots. To cope with its expansion, the hospital bought an undeveloped hundred-acre tract on the western edge of Winchester in 1983 for a new hospital site.

Dr. William Janney Best of Brucetown makes a house call circa 1890 at Pidgeon's Bottom near Wadesville in Clarke County. He was born in 1834 and died in 1908. Courtesy of his granddaughter, Dakota Janney Best Brown

Winchester Memorial Hospital, Winchester, Va.

Winchester Medical Center began as Winchester Memorial Hospital in this building at Clifford and Stewart streets. It opened officially on March 17, 1903, but got its first patient on March 26, 1902, when Pompey Green, a black construction worker who was injured in a fight, was taken there. The original hospital of thirty-six beds has since expanded to cover an entire block with a number of nearby parking lots. The hospital treated 5,153 patients in 1945 and 6,954 in 1946. In 1987, 91,318 patients were admitted to the hospital and there were 90,000 outpatients. It was licensed for 442 beds and averaged 250 patients per day in 1988. Courtesy of the Winchester Star

The new Winchester Medical Center at Amherst Street and Va. 37 while under construction in February 1988. The six-floor, 340-bed hospital should be finished in July 1989, with personnel and equipment moving into the new facility in August 1989. Costing fifty-two million dollars, it is the largest construction project in the city's history. It will replace the hospital on Stewart Street. Also under construction at the site is a four-story, eighty-million-dollar medical office building and cancer care center. The project is being financed with $86.5 million in tax-exempt industrial development bonds that cover the cost of the two new facilities, refinancing previous debts, and relocation. Also shown is the Surgi-Center of Winchester, which opened in 1985 and performed its ten-thousandth operation on March 17, 1988, and the Diagnostic Imaging Center, which opened in 1986. The Surgi-Center is east of the new hospital, the Diagnostic Imaging Center is west of it, and the medical offices are on the south. Photo by Rudy Rodgers of Birds-Eye View

The Anti-Saloon League gathered on the steps of the old Frederick County Courthouse just before a parade in April 1908. More than five hundred women and a number of Shenandoah Military Academy cadets marched down Main Street (now the Loudoun Street Mall) in support of a referendum to ban liquor in Winchester. The drys won by one hundred votes. Courtesy of the Winchester-Frederick County Historical Society

Turn-of-the-century inventions and early twentieth-century events have forever changed the way we live. Thomas Edison brought us electric lights and telephones, Henry Ford marketed the first automobile in the 1890s, and aviation was born when the Wright Brothers flew their airplane at Kitty Hawk, North Carolina, on December 17, 1903.

Local telephone service began in 1885. Electricity came to Winchester in 1889 and to Stephens City in 1915. In the early twentieth century, electricity was extended to sections of Frederick County where customers signed up for service. Some rural sections did not get power lines until the 1940s.

There was a grass airstrip on the eastern edge of Winchester by the late 1920s, and fliers performing aerobatic stunts were a familiar site in the 1930s. Trains remained an important means of transportation. The Winchester & Western Railroad was completed in 1921.

Women got the right to vote in 1920. Isabell Baker became the first woman in Winchester to register. Blacks in Virginia got the right to vote in 1869, the same year the secret ballot was adopted, but literacy tests and a poll tax imposed in 1901 and not voided until the 1960s effectively disenfranchised many black and poor, uneducated white voters.

Company I of the 116th U.S. Infantry marched in the World War I Victory Parade through downtown Winchester in 1919. Courtesy of the Handley Library Archives

Prohibition did not survive but it found strong support in the Shenandoah Valley and Virginia long before the twentieth amendment to the U.S. Constitution banned liquor nationwide in 1919. The Virginia General Assembly passed the Byrd Liquor Law more than a decade before, which banned alcohol sales to minors and allowed localities to outlaw liquor. Many Northern Shenandoah Valley towns took advantage of the opportunity to go dry, making Harrisonburg the only alcoholic oasis between Staunton and Harpers Ferry, West Virginia.

The Virginia Anti-Saloon League, a powerful force in Virginia politics at the beginning of the twentieth century, had an organization in Winchester. There also was an active chapter of the Women's Christian Temperance Union at the Braddock Street United Methodist Church.

Famous saloon-buster Carrie Nation drew crowds when she spoke in Winchester in April 1908. During a walk through downtown, according to the *Winchester Evening Star*, she lectured a young man she saw smoking a cigarette, calling him an "imp" when he refused to stop.

Nation, who had built a reputation for smashing saloons with an ax, only gave out commemorative gold and rhinestone hatchets to local newspaper reporters during her visit. She did not have to resort to violence. On April 15, 1908, Winchester residents had voted to ban liquor, forcing eleven local bars to close by May 1. The measure passed by 100 votes; 832 were cast. More than five hundred women, including members of the Anti-Saloon League, and a number of Shenandoah Military Academy cadets paraded down Loudoun Street in support of the local prohibition.

Men from Frederick County and Winchester fought in the two world wars. Locally the Great Depression hit hard. Adm. Richard E. Byrd, a Winchester native, gave the country something to cheer about when he led the first flight over the South Pole on November 29, 1929, exactly one month after Black Tuesday, the day the stock market crashed.

The Japanese bombed Pearl Harbor on December 7, 1941. In the months that followed, local defense units were organized and volunteers manned lookout towers in Winchester and Frederick County to spot enemy aircraft before they attacked. In February 1942, the Chesapeake & Potomac Telephone Company installed an air raid warning system at the Winchester Police Department, men between the ages of twenty and forty-four were required to register for the draft, and the whistle at the O'Sullivan Corporation was rebuilt for air raid warnings.

By March 1942, local restaurants were rationing sugar and in May, nightly blackouts began to protect local people from feared aerial attacks. Soon gasoline and alcohol were rationed and pleasure driving was banned. In January 1943 area residents were told by a spokesman for the local gasoline rationing board to limit hospital visits to patients who were close relatives.

The war had escalated by 1944 and so did local efforts. Hundreds of thousands of dollars in war bonds were sold locally, including more than three hundred thousand dollars in bonds that Winchester, Virginia residents bought by August 1944 to win a friendly competition with Winchester, Massachusetts. In September 1944, 350 captured German soldiers were housed at a prisoner-of-war camp in Winchester. In October 1944 the Corcoran Gallery of Washington, D.C., stored three million dollars worth of art treasures for safekeeping in the basement of Handley High School and left them there for two years.

CERTIFICATE OF REGISTRATION SINCE JANUARY 1, 1904.

VIRGINIA: COUNTY OF *Frederick*

The undersigned Registrar for *Registrar* .... Precinct,

in *Stonewall* .... Magisterial District, in the said County,

hereby certifies that the person herein named is duly registered on the list of voters registered since Jan. 1, 1904 in said precinct, in said Magisterial District, as follows, viz: Date of Registration *Oct 2* 19 *20*

Color *W* No. *5* Name *Fannie B. Dunlap*

Date of Birth *Mch. 25/1864* Age *56* years, Occupation *Housewife*

Place of Residence *Berryville Pike* .... Length of Residence in State *56* years,

County *56* Precinct *56* ; if naturalized, Date of Papers ....

.... Issued by .... Court of ...., and is

registered as* *not* exempt from payment of poll tax as a prerequisite to the right to vote. This certificate is given to enable the person named to change his place of voting to .... Precinct, in

2nd ~~Ward~~, of the ~~City~~ ~~District~~ County of *Winchester Va*

and that his name has been erased from the registration books of the precinct first above named.

Date this *Feb 13* ...., 19 *22* *C. Richard Boyce*

*Note.—If NOT exempt, insert the word "not" in this blank. Registrar.

Women got the right to vote in 1920 but in Virginia they had to pay a poll tax and fill out a form that required them to give their age. Prognosticators predicted that women would sacrifice their newly won suffrage rather than tell how old they were. Women proved them wrong and signed up anyway, including Fannie B. Dunlap, a fifty-six-year-old housewife who lived on Berryville Pike (Va. 7) and filled out this voter registration form. From the Gibson Baker Collection; courtesy of the Winchester-Frederick County History Society

When the Winchester & Western Railroad was completed on May 25, 1921, the area's leading residents celebrated with a luncheon at the end of the line in Wardensville, West Virginia. A special train brought 350 people from Winchester to attend the event. John J. Cornwell, a former governor of West Virginia and brother of the railroad's president, spoke.

Those in this photograph whose identities are known are, standing, W & W president

William B. Cornwell, far left; vice president Herbert S. Larrick, second from left; Spot White, fourth from left, and Harold Sheetz, fifth from left. Doug Fuller, standing toward the right, is wearing a hat. Stewart Bell, Sr., is seated third from left and Russell Cather is seated tenth from left.

It took four years to lay the forty miles of track between Winchester and Wardensville.

The railroad was expected to hasten the development of the region's timber and natural resources by providing a fast route to Winchester, which had a connection to the Baltimore & Ohio Railroad. Before the W & W, the only way to transport timber from the region was over wagon roads. The railroad also offered passenger service. Courtesy of the Winchester-Frederick County Historical Society

This railbus, the No. 10, carried passengers and farm products. It was the first one in service after the Winchester & Western Railroad's line from Winchester to Wardensville, West Virginia, was completed in May 1821. The vehicle consisted of a bus body mounted on a chassis and steel tires. It pulled a four-wheel trailer, which also is shown here. The conductor and engineer, above, were stopped near the campgrounds at Wardensville. Courtesy of the Winchester-Frederick County Historical Society

Operators at the Chesapeake & Potomac Telephone Company in Winchester circa 1935. Telephone service began locally in 1885 with the Winchester Telephone Company. It began with thirty-five customers who paid about ten cents a day for service, and there were predictions that service would soon be extended to Stephens City, Middletown, Brucetown, and Berryville. The company lasted until 1904. It did not submit a bid to renew its franchise, and the City Council awarded the franchise to Southern Bell Telephone Company, which had hired Harry F. Byrd, Sr., as its local superintendent. Southern Bell promised to soon provide long-distance service, and the first long-distance calls were made on July 26, 1904, to Staunton, Richmond, and Atlanta, Georgia. The Winchester Jordan Springs Telephone Company was created in 1905 and the two companies competed for eight years. In 1913, C & P superseded Southern Bell and bought the Winchester Jordan Springs Company and the Winchester Nineoch Telephone Company, which operated lines in Frederick and Warren counties. After the consolidation, C & P provided service to 1,000 customers. There were 3,500 by 1940; 6,981 by 1950; 11,393 by 1960; 19,111 by 1970; and 27,070 by 1978. In 1988 there were seven local exchanges and 30,736 access lines. Courtesy of Winchester-Frederick County Historical Society

A bond drive was held circa 1944 in front of McCrory's Ten Cent Store in Winchester. Local people spent hundreds of thousands of dollars to finance the American effort during World War II by buying war bonds. Courtesy of the Winchester-Frederick County Historical Society

Dr. Benjamin B. Dutton, Sr., and his wife, Ann, prepare for the christening of the S.S. Winchester Victory, a World War II merchant marine ship, on March 6, 1945, in Baltimore, Maryland. Ann Dutton, who headed numerous wartime projects on the home-front, cracked a bottle of champagne across the ship's bow amid the cheers of shipyard workers and fifty Winchester residents before the 450-foot-long ship slid into the waters of the Patapsco River. WINC radio also broadcast the christening. The ship had been built in forty-seven days by the Bethlehem-Fairfield Shipyard in Baltimore and was one of many Victory cargo ships built to carry supplies to soldiers fighting overseas. The ship was named in Winchester's honor after city residents donated books for the ship's library.

It is not known whether the ship was ever fired upon when it was refitted four months later as a troop carrier for duty in the Pacific, but its maiden voyage to Marseilles, France, was merry. The war in Europe had ended and the sailors arrived just in time to help the French celebrate Allied victory. The ship was sold to the Netherlands in 1957. Courtesy of Benjamin B. Dutton, Jr.

The Jack Fretwell Orchestra, a local band, plays at Yorks Inn in the late 1940s. Fretwell is at the microphone. George York ran the dance hall and motel with his wife from 1934 until his death in 1942. He had served under Gen. George A. Custer and was one of ten men on leave when the famous Indian fighter made his last stand.

In its heyday, Yorks was the place to be seen. Alfred deMazzon, a native of Venice, Italy, and manager of the Carlton Hotel in Washington, D.C., bought the inn after York died and decorated it with antiques, a fountain at the entrance, and caged exotic birds in the lobby. The inn, on U.S. 11 at Welltown Pike, burned to the ground in 1961. Courtesy of the Winchester Star

Harry Flood Byrd, Sr., was Virginia's political patriarch for forty years. He built the Democratic Party into a force that controlled politics from the courthouse to the capital. Born in Martinsburg, West Virginia, in 1887, he was elected to the Winchester City Council when he was twenty-one years old, became a state senator when he was twenty-seven, was elected governor when he was thirty-eight, and became a U.S. senator when he was forty-five, serving thirty-two years, longer than anyone else in the state's history.

A direct descendant of William Byrd II, the founder of Richmond, Byrd was raised on politics and newspapers. His father, Richard Evelyn Byrd, was speaker of the Virginia House of Delegates and his uncle, Hal Flood, was a member of the U.S. House of Representatives. He left school at the age of fifteen to run his father's newspaper, the Winchester Evening Star, which was near bankruptcy. He turned the paper around and took a second job as a telephone company manager and used his earnings to start buying apple orchards. He eventually became one of the world's largest apple growers and built the Winchester Cold Storage, the biggest apple storage facility of its time.

Byrd became chairman of the state Democratic Party in 1922, which put him in position to shape the party and get Democrats elected to office. In 1923, he helped defeat a state highway bond referendum and was the architect of the pay-as-you-go philosophy that has dominated state government in the twentieth century. Under his urging, the General Assembly passed a gasoline tax of three cents a gallon.

When Byrd became governor in 1926, he streamlined government and consolidated power by reducing the number of statewide elected officials and the number of state agencies. He was responsible for the establishment of Shenandoah National Park and persuaded the legislature to pass an anti-lynching law in 1928. When he took office, the state was in debt; when he left, it had a surplus of more than four million dollars. The term "massive resistance" was coined when Byrd, responding to the U.S. Supreme Court's decision that ended segregated schools, said, "Massive resistance is the best course for us to take." Some school systems in the state shut down rather than integrate.

Byrd was appointed to the Senate in 1933 and won election five times. As chairman of the Finance Committee, he opposed many of the New Deal policies of President Franklin D. Roosevelt. He resigned in 1965 because of poor health and died the following year. His son, Harry F. Byrd, Jr., was appointed to his seat. From the John Walter Wayland Collection; courtesy of the Winchester-Frederick County Historical Society

Virginia Gov. Harry F. Byrd, Sr. (center), is seen here with his son, Harry F. Byrd, Jr., a future senator, dressed in the uniform of a member of the governor's staff, and his brother, orchardist Thomas B. Byrd. This photograph was taken circa 1927 in Richmond. The two Byrd brothers were among the largest apple growers in the world. Courtesy of the Virginia Historical Society

Adm. Richard Evelyn Byrd, shown here with his Antarctic companion, Igloo, was the first man to fly over the North and South poles and the first to fly a multi-engined plane over the Atlantic. He brought aviation and modern communications to polar exploration, which had been limited to men on dogsleds, and chartered more than two million square miles of the earth's surface.

Born in Winchester in 1888, he grew up on Amherst Street and later lived in Boston. He was named for his father, publisher of the *Winchester Evening Star*. His brother was Harry F. Byrd, Sr.

Byrd and Floyd Bennett flew over the North Pole on May 9, 1926. Byrd and his chief pilot, Bernt Balchen, flew over the South Pole on November 29, 1929. He launched a second Antarctic expedition in 1933. He lived alone at an advance base camp and nearly died from carbon monoxide poisoning in 1934 when he was forced to continue using a malfunctioning stove so he would not freeze to death. His brush with death was the subject of his 1934 book, *Alone*.

Byrd headed Operation Highjump in 1946-1947 and made his second flight over the South Pole on February 16, 1947. The largest expedition to Antarctica, it photographed much of the continent's coast for the first time and included the discovery of mountain ranges. Byrd again visited Antarctica in 1955 and 1956 and flew over the South Pole a third time before he died in 1957. Courtesy of the National Archives

Adm. Richard E. Byrd Field was established about 1930 with grass strip runways southeast of U.S. 50 and 522 in Frederick County, where Delco Plaza is today. It preceded Winchester Regional Airport on Bufflick Road as the area's aviation facility. This photo was taken circa 1932 by Frank Turgeon, a World War I photographer who later took aerial photographs for Pan-American Airways. Turgeon helped to promote shows for local barnstormers in the 1930s. Courtesy of Catherine A. Scheder

Local Aviation

The origins of aviation in Frederick County can be traced to a 1920s grass airstrip southeast of U.S. 50 and 522 in Frederick County that was named Adm. Richard E. Byrd Field about 1930. Aviation was still in its infancy when barnstormers such as George Scheder, Duke Douglas, and Squeek Burnett came to town in the early 1930s. They called themselves the Angels From Hell and performed daredevil aerobatic stunts, such as flying upside down and making dead-motor landings from three thousand feet.

C. Herbert Shutte owned Byrd Field and was its first manager. About 1933, he hired Scheder, who also was an airplane mechanic, to manage flying operations at the field, which then had a small office, hangar, and runways of mowed grass.

Within a few years, traffic increased at Byrd Field. Scheder persuaded Winchester to lease 129 acres along Bufflick Road (State Route 645) on October 7, 1936, and the city exercised an option to buy the property on November 24, 1943. The airport has since grown to 226 acres.

Winchester Municipal Airport was officially recognized by Virginia as a licensed commercial airport on December 2, 1937; and Valley Airways Inc., an aviation business that Scheder started with the financial backing of Paul Rosenberger and other local businessmen, was hired to operate the facility, with Scheder as its manager. The airport soon offered a Civilian Pilot Training Program, which was suspended when civilian flights were stopped during World War II, and later offered War Training Service for servicemen about to begin military flight training.

Scheder was succeeded as airport manager in 1955 by Donald Patton, who persuaded local businesses in 1961 to contribute money to pave and light a runway thirty-six hundred feet long. It was later expanded to a five thousand-foot airplane taxiway that is parallel to the airport's current runway of forty-five hundred feet.

Over the years other companies were hired to run the airport, including Skyline Aviation, which briefly offered commuter airline service in 1976. The city hired Bill Sager as airport manager in 1982. He retired in 1985 and was killed in a 1987 airplane crash in Florida. Kenneth F. Wiegand, a retired military flier, replaced Sager.

The Winchester Regional Airport Commission was created as an advisory board to the city in July 1983, with members serving from Winchester and Frederick and

George Scheder, the manager of Byrd Field, became the first manager of Winchester Municipal Airport when it opened on Bufflick Road in 1936. He served until 1955 and later opened Valley Photo on the Loudoun Street Mall.

Scheder was born in the Bronx in 1910 and died in 1972. He was drawn to aviation when Charles A. Lindbergh flew solo over the Atlantic Ocean, enrolled in aviation school in 1929, and bought a bimotor airplane. While still in New York, he and Duke Douglas teamed up as flying partners. They started out as weekend fliers, giving air shows in small towns in New York and New Jersey and offering dollar rides. Douglas did most of the stunts and Scheder, who also flew, was the mechanic and businessman.

They started moving south in the summer of of 1930 and began working for weeks at a time, with Scheder driving ahead in a Model T Ford to promote upcoming air shows before Douglas flew into town. One of their first shows at Byrd Field was called "The Trail of Pink Petals" in which they sprinkled confetti over the city during the 1931 Shenandoah Apple Blossom Festival. They later joined other barnstormer fliers in putting on shows and called themselves the Angels From Hell.

Scheder was hired to manage Byrd Field by its owner and previous manager, C. Herbert Shutte, and joined local businessmen in forming Valley Airways, a charter aviation company that made an unsuccessful attempt to offer scheduled commuter flights. The company later ran the airport. Courtesy of his wife, Catherine A. Scheder

Mary Elizabeth "Teedie" Ebert became the Winchester area's first female pilot just before World War II. She was twenty-two when this photograph appeared in the Winchester Evening Star. She made national news when her picture and story were carried by the Associated Press.

She married Hamil Jones not long after she learned to fly and now lives in Richmond. She was the only woman enrolled in the Civilian Pilot Training Program at Shepherd College in Shepherdstown, West Virginia, from the fall of 1940 to the spring of 1941.

"It was right before Pearl Harbor," Mary Jones recalled. The war cut into her flying because the government revoked all civilian pilot licenses and only allowed the military to fly airplanes. Jones is shown in front of a Piper Cub that she flew. The propeller had to be turned to start, and some of the planes she flew did not have brakes.

Jones was the last principal of Brucetown School, which closed in 1941. She was then assistant principal at Stonewall School before she joined the Intelligence Department of the U.S. Signal Corp. Courtesy of Catherine A. Scheder

Clarke counties. A General Assembly Act created the Winchester Regional Airport Authority on July 1, 1987. Airport operations and the facility were turned over to the independent authority and the name of the facility was changed to Winchester Regional Airport. Today the authority also includes representatives from Warren and Shenandoah counties.

In 1988 the airport put into operation an instrument landing approach system that allows airplanes to land in bad weather by relying on instruments. The authority also approved a $7.2-million budget for capital improvements for 1988-1993 that includes a terminal to replace the one that was built in sections beginning in 1936, extension of the runway to fifty-five hundred feet, additional parking for airplanes and automobiles, an access road to the terminal, and more hangars. Also in 1988, work began on a project to relocate Bufflick Road to allow airport expansion and to extend water and sewer lines to the airport and nearby industrial parks.

Two views of Winchester Municipal Airport in the 1950s. The terminal was built in stages beginning with the east hangar soon after Winchester leased land for the airport in 1936 and ending with the construction of offices in the 1950s. The building is scheduled for replacement in 1989 by a larger facility just south (right) of the older building. In 1988, a 1.2 mile stretch of Bufflick Road, shown in the aerial photo, also was relocated south (right) of where it is shown here. Photo of terminal by Arthur Belt; aerial courtesy of Catherine A. Scheder

Schools

From the eighteenth century until Virginia's current public education system began in 1870, there were more than fifty private schools in Winchester, including academies for boys and seminaries for women, and at least another fifty field schools in Frederick County. Wealthy families also sometimes hired tutors or governesses. The earliest evidence of a school in Winchester is a 1748 entry in the journal of Col. James Wood, the founder of Winchester.

An 1818 General Assembly act provided funds for indigent children to study at private schools, but attendance was low. There had always been opposition to public schools in Virginia, especially among large land-owners who feared the poor would become empowered by education. Others simply did not want to pay for it.

After the public school system began in Virginia, Frederick County was divided into five districts with the same names as its current magisterial districts, and trustees were appointed to run the schools and collect taxes for them. The General Assembly replaced the system with school boards in 1922.

A. M. Smith was named the first superintendent of schools in Winchester and Frederick and Clarke counties in 1870 and was replaced the following year by the Rev. H. S. Phillips, who also served one year. The three localities had the same school system until Winchester separated from the Frederick County system in 1919. Clarke remained part of the county school system until 1929.

William H. Gold, a Stonewall District trustee, was appointed school superintendent in 1872 and remained for eleven years. He was succeeded by two superintendents with short administrations—A. M. Pierce, who was appointed by a local judge in 1883 but was not confirmed by the state senate, and George W. Ward, who was confirmed in 1884.

Four strong superintendents then ran the system for almost a century. The first was Maurice M. Lynch, who was appointed superintendent in 1888 and served for twenty-nine years. An attorney and president of the Winchester Bar Association, he was born in 1854 and died in 1944. During his administration, the first county high schools opened, at Middletown in 1909 and Stephens City in 1914.

Lynch was followed by Leslie D. Kline, the longest serving superintendent. Kline was appointed in 1917. During his thirty-two-year tenure, the system experienced dramatic change. Small schools were replaced with

William H. Gold was superintendent of Frederick County schools from 1872 to 1883. He is said to have worked tirelessly for public education and used to ride through the county on horseback to inspect the schools. He also was a school trustee and a member of the School Board. Born in 1820, he lived on Gold's Hill on Apple Pie Ridge and died in 1898. He was the father of twelve children. His daughter, Laura Gold Crawford, was the co-founder of Fort Loudoun Seminary, a women's school at the site of old Fort Loudoun in Winchester that she started in 1905 with Katherine Glass Greene. His son, Philip H. Gold, was a prominent apple grower and clerk of the Circuit Court. Courtesy of the Frederick County School Board Office

large, modern facilities and more high schools opened—Gainesboro in 1935, Gore in 1938, and Stonewall in 1941.

Kline also planned a modern facility that would house all high school students in Frederick County. The result was James Wood High School. When it opened in 1950, the county's five high schools became elementary schools. Of those schools, only Stonewall remains in operation today. Stephens City closed in 1975 and was replaced by Bass-Hoover Elementary School; Middletown closed in 1983 and school zones were changed to make room for its students at Bass-Hoover; Gore and Gainesboro were replaced in 1988 by Indian Hollow Elementary School, a new facility on State Route 600. A new Middletown Elementary School is being built on U.S. 11. The two new facilities will be capable of holding up to 625 students each.

Public schools in Frederick County were segregated until the 1960s. The first fully integrated school was Frederick County Junior High, which opened in 1965. It now is a middle school.

Robert E. Aylor taught students at Stephens City for twenty-two years before becoming superintendent of Frederick County's public school system in 1949. Born in Chatham, Virginia, in 1903, he graduated from the University of Virginia in 1925, was hired that year as a math teacher at Stephens City High School, and soon became principal of the school and coach of its baseball team. He earned a master's degree from the University of Virginia by taking summer courses. As superintendent, Aylor moved forward with Kline's plans for consolidation. Eight smaller schools were replaced by six larger ones; additions were built to Stonewall, Gainesboro, and Gore elementary schools; the old Miller School on Whitlock Avenue was converted to administrative offices; and plans were made for a second junior high school and Dowell J. Howard Vocational Center. Aylor retired in 1968. Robert E. Aylor Middle School east of Stephens City is named after him. Courtesy of the Frederick County School Board Office

Melton F. Wright was superintendent of Frederick County schools from 1968 until his retirement in 1982. He was born in 1922 in Charleston, South Carolina, and began his teaching career in Frederick County in 1945. Wright received a bachelor's degree and honorary doctorate of laws from Bob Jones University and a master's degree from the University of Virginia. He was principal of several schools, including Boyce Agricultural School in Clarke County and Harrisonburg High School, before returning to Frederick County in 1958 as director of instruction. He became assistant superintendent in 1965 and was promoted to superintendent three years later. Wright also was president of the Winchester Easter Seal Society and the United Fund and was the weekend minister at Rockland Community Church in Warren County for more than twenty years. He wrote six books and numerous newspaper and magazine articles on education and religion. He died in 1983. Courtesy of the Winchester Star

The call for better facilities for black students began in the late 1950s, when black parents asked the school board to provide a consolidated school to replace three one-room schoolhouses in Stephens City, Middletown, and Cedar Hill in Clearbrook. They were the only schools where blacks were taught in Frederick County and they did not have running water or electricity. The result of the black parents's efforts was Gibson Elementary School, a four-room facility at the end of Smithfield Avenue that was named for Powell W. Gibson, the first principal of Douglas School (then Winchester's all-black school and now Frederick Douglass Elementary School). The old Gibson School now houses the Northwestern Regional Education Program.

The desegregation movement in Frederick County

began in 1962, when Julian E. Brown of Clearbrook requested that his six children be allowed to attend white schools. He was turned down and filed a suit against the School Board in U.S. District Court.

Integration began in 1964, when the School Board adopted a freedom of choice plan that allowed black parents whose children were about to enter a school for the first time to decide whether to send their children to Gibson Elementary School or a white school. Black students who went on to high school still attended Douglas School.

Later that year, after the School Board lost the lawsuit to Brown, the board adopted an integration policy that assigned students to schools based on their geographical area and not their race.

Kenneth E. Walker became schools super-intendent in 1982. He was born in 1936 in Old Fort, North Carolina, and is a former English instructor and assistant professor at Virginia Tech. He also taught at Mercer University in Macon, Georgia, and at secondary schools in New Jersey and North Carolina. He was super-intendent of Northumberland County public schools for four years before he came to Frederick County. Walker earned a doctorate from the University of Georgia, a master's degree from Wake Forest University, and a bachelor's degree from Mercer University. He has given speeches at four national education conferences, including one at the 1987 U.S. Department of Education National Conference on Drug-Free Schools, at which he outlined Winchester and Frederick County's drug-abuse prevention program. Photo by Ray K. Saunders; courtesy of the Winchester Star

Since public schools began, enrollment in Frederick County Schools has nearly tripled, while the number of schools has declined with the move from small neighborhood schools to large, consolidated facilities.

When Schools Superintendent Gold filed his first report in 1872, there were 2,455 students enrolled out of a school age population of 5,216. There were fifty-five schools in Winchester and Frederick and Clarke counties. There were sixty-one teachers and their average monthly pay was $27.30. By 1886, there were between seventy-five and eighty schools in Frederick County alone.

In 1967, 6,590 students were enrolled in Frederick County schools. The number increased to 7,366 by 1970 but fell to 6,724 in 1972 after Winchester annexed portions of the county. Enrollment increased to 7,320 in 1973, when kindergarten began, grew to 7,775 by 1976, but fell between 1977 and 1984. The school population is once again on the rise, growing from 6,949 in 1982 to 7,402 in 1987.

Dowell Jennings Howard, the state superintend-ent of Virginia public schools from 1949 until his death in 1957, began his teaching career in Boyce and Winchester. He helped organize the Future Farmers of Virginia and the Future Farmers of America, and was the national group's treasurer. Dowell J. Howard Vocational-Technical Center, a public school for students in Winchester and Frederick and Clarke counties, is named in his honor.

Howard was born in 1894 in Brookeville, Maryland. He received bachelor's and master's degrees from the University of Maryland and studied at Virginia Tech. After serving in World War I, he became a vocational agricul-ture instructor at Boyce High School in Clarke County in 1919 and the school's principal in 1924. He also organized the Clarke County Farmers Association.

He became district supervisor of agricultural education for Northern Virginia in 1926 and had an office in Winchester. Howard remained until his appointment as acting state supervisor of agricultural education in 1942. In 1934-1935 he was president of the Winchester Rotary Club.

Howard became assistant state supervisor of public instruction in 1946, was named acting superintendent in 1949, and was chosen per-manent superintendent in 1950. Portrait by Steve Rosenberger; courtesy of Dowell J. Howard Vocational-Technical Center.

Frederick County once had five high schools. These are a few of their yearbooks. Middletown, Stephens City, Gore, Gainesboro, and Stonewall high schools became elementary schools after James Wood High School opened in 1950. Courtesy of the Frederick County School Board Office

James Wood High School on Amherst Street was Frederick County's first consolidated high school. It opened in 1950 and had ninety people in its first graduating class, in 1951. Additions were built in 1963 and 1971. It was replaced as the county's senior high school when James Wood High School-Ridge Campus opened in 1981; it now houses students in grades nine and ten.

The school is named for Col. James Wood,

the founder of Winchester. It is next to Wood's estate, Glen Burnie, and was built on thirty acres that were part of the original farm. It held grades five through twelve as late as 1956, grades seven through twelve after 1957, and grades ten through twelve after Frederick County Junior High School opened in 1965. Photo by Rich Cooley; courtesy of the Northern Virginia Daily

James Wood High School on Apple Pie Ridge opened in January 1981. It houses all of Frederick County's students in grades eleven and twelve and has a capacity for 1,350 students. There were 358 students in the school's first graduating class in 1981 and 524 graduates in the class of 1988.

The school was built on a site of sixty-eight acres off U.S. 522 north of Winchester and cost more than ten million dollars, about three million dollars more than originally estimated. Additional money had to be allocated for practice athletic fields, which where added after the school was built: the Board of Supervisors has also committed one million dollars to build a stadium in 1989. Photo by Teresa Lazazzera

Ground was broken on April 4, 1987, for Mary M. Henkel Hall, the home of the Harry F. Byrd, Jr. School of Business at Shenandoah College and Conservatory; the $1.5 million building was dedicated on March 19, 1988. Mary Henkel, the chairman of the board of Henkel-Harris Corporation, and Byrd, a former U.S. senator, are shown unearthing the first shovels of dirt while Shenandoah president James A. Davis, a former state delegate, left, and James R. Wilkins, Sr., look on. The business school opened in 1984. Photo by Roger Hendrix; courtesy of the Winchester Star

Shenandoah College and Conservatory students performing at the Dorothy Ewing Studio of Dance Art, which opened in 1988. It is named for a ballerina who became Winchester's first professional dance instructor and who spent more than thirty-seven years teaching ballet, tap, jazz, and ballroom dancing before she retired in 1971. The state-of-the-art dance studio is in an addition to the Shingleton Building. It has a nine-layer basket-weave floor that is designed to reduce injuries by providing a surface with "give." Photo by Scott Mason; courtesy of the Winchester Star

Shenandoah College and Conservatory opened in Winchester on September 15, 1960. It relocated from cramped quarters in Dayton, Virginia, where the private school was established in 1875, to a thirty-acre site off Millwood Avenue at the eastern edge of Winchester. Its holdings have since grown to sixty-seven acres, including eighteen acres of undeveloped land east of the school in Frederick County and old John Kerr School at Cork and Cameron streets. Enrollment was 198 students in 1959, the last year the school was in Dayton, and had grown to 330 when the school opened in Winchester the following year. It then was a junior college with a conservatory that offered a bachelor's degree in music. It now is a four-year liberal arts college that also has business and nursing schools and offers master's degrees in business administration, music education, conducting, composition, and performance. There were 971 students enrolled in the fall of 1987 and enrollment is projected to reach 1,200 in the 1990s.

James R. Wilkins, Sr., and his wife, Mary, who died in 1987, have been major contributors to Shenandoah College and Conservatory. Wilkins, a former Winchester councilman and founder of Wilkins ShoeCenter, was instrumental in bringing Shenandoah to Winchester.

He was president of the Winchester-Frederick County Chamber of Commerce when it approached the school in 1955 about moving to Winchester. He is the author of The Impossible Task, a history of Shenandoah published in 1985. Courtesy of James R. Wilkins, Sr.

William H. McCoy, the founding president of Lord Fairfax Community College, stands in front of the Old Dominion Motel north of Middletown where the school's first office was located in 1969. "It was a sparse beginning," McCoy said. "The building was not ready."

LFCC still was not finished when it opened for classes the following year. The windows had not been measured correctly and were not installed until later in the term. Desks rounded up from other community colleges did not arrive until the first day of class.

McCoy was LFCC's president until he resigned in 1987 to become president of North Florida Junior College. Marilyn C. Beck took his place, becoming the second female community college president in Virginia. She is a former dean at Lurleen B. Wallace State Junior College in Andalusia, Alabama. Courtesy of Lord Fairfax Community College

Lord Fairfax Community College has grown from 570 students when it opened on September 28, 1970, to an enrollment of 2,254 students in the fall of 1987. A regional college for the Northern Shenandoah Valley, it is located on 101 acres on U.S. 11 just north of Middletown. The school is part of the Virginia Community College system created in 1966 by Gov. Mills E. Godwin as a low-cost alternative to four-year colleges. LFCC is a two-year college that offers associate degrees. Nearly all its students are part-time. More than one-third of its students transfer to four-year colleges.

This is Lord Fairfax Community College as it looks today. Photo by Scott Mason; courtesy of the Winchester Star

Business and Industry

Nicki and Joe Zuckerman stand in front of the original office of L. Zuckerman and Sons, where the couple met. Zuckerman and his brothers, Sam, Irvin, Charles, and Aaron, operated the scrap metal and recycling company with their father, Louis, a Russian Jewish immigrant who came to the United States in 1905 and to Winchester in 1917. Over the years the brothers split up the business, and now Joe operates the scrap division, which accepts metal castoffs, processes them, and ships them to foundries to be turned into new metal products. The original business was on Baker Street in Winchester and then moved to Kent Street before moving to U.S. 11 in the 1960s. The old office made the move each time and now is opposite the company headquarters. Nicki Zuckerman is a former nurse. Photo by Susan Burke; courtesy of the Winchester Star

Business and industrial corridors began developing in Frederick County on U.S. 11 along the northern and southern entrances to Winchester in the early and mid-twentieth century. They also developed in Winchester along North Cameron Street and North Loudoun Street. In the nineteenth century, Frederick County had a variety of industries, such as the tannery at Star Tannery and a flour and feed mill at Middletown. Quarry operations, such as the M. J. Grove Lime Company in Stephens City and Stuart M. Perry Quarry on old Route 50, also began in the early twentieth century.

Among major manufacturers in Winchester and Frederick County today is the O'Sullivan Corporation on Valley Avenue, a plastics manufacturer with fifteen hundred workers. Opening in 1932 as a manufacturer of rubber heels and soles, today it manufactures vinyl sheeting for everything from automobile instrument and door panels and bumpers to shower curtains, handbags, and checkbook covers. Abex Corporation, a manufacturer of brake linings and other automotive products, opened a plant on Paper Mill Road in 1947 and today employs more than six hundred people. General Electric, which opened an incandescent lamp plant at Kernstown in 1975, employs 550 people and produces more than a million light bulbs a day. Rubbermaid also has a plant in Winchester with more than six hundred employees. National Fruit Products Company, a fruit processor, has more than eight hundred employees; and Capital Records, which closed in 1988, at one time had seven hundred employees. More than five hundred people work at Crown Cork & Seal Company on U.S. 11 north of Winchester; it is the largest manufacturing plant for easy-open aluminum can tops in the world.

Western Union, south of Middletown, has more than one hundred employees. Every money order Western Union processes in the United States—between thirty thousand and fifty thousand a day—is relayed through the Middletown office.

In 1860, there were 127 established businesses in Winchester and Frederick County, including thirty-seven flour and grist mills, twenty-six lumber businesses, seven companies that manufactured woolen goods, and three glove makers. By 1880, many businesses had merged or gone out of business, reducing the number to fifty-one.

In 1984, there were 1,243 established businesses in Winchester and 226 more in Frederick County. Of those, 458 were service businesses, 411 were retail, 131 were finance, insurance, and real estate, 108 were contract construction, and 68 were manufacturing.

In 1988, there were at least seventeen industrial sites in Winchester and Frederick County. Two of the sites are industrial parks totaling nearly five hundred acres next to Winchester Regional Airport. Much of Winchester's remaining industrial and commercial development is expected to occur along vacant land on Pleasant Valley Road.

The Shockey Companies on U.S. 11 north of
Winchester were pioneers in the concrete and
construction businesses. This is Shockey
Brothers's first casting yard for prestressed,
precast concrete products in the late 1950s.

The companies trace their roots to Howard
Shockey, who built stagecoaches at a shop on
Fairfax Lane. He got into the construction business about the time automobiles began replacing
wagons. He had begun building houses by 1896
and opened the business that became Howard
Shockey & Son, a general contracting firm, on
Charles Street off Fairview Avenue in 1907. In
1943, James Crider, a former barrel manufacturer, and Howard Shockey's son, James
Shockey, Sr., formed Crider & Shockey, a
ready-mix concrete business, and opened an
office on U.S. 11 north of Winchester. James
Shockey, Sr., continued the business when
Crider died in 1949. In 1954, he and his
brothers also began making precast concrete and
incorporated as Shockey Brothers in 1959. Courtesy of the Shockey Companies

Crown Cork & Seal on U.S. 11 north of Winchester opened for business on October 30, 1959.
Bruce Whitacre, a long-time worker and a
Frederick County resident, maintains the
machines that form one-gallon tin cans. A
former agriculture teacher at Handley High
School, he had worked at the plant for twenty-
seven years when this photograph was taken in
1986. Tin cans, which now account for about
10 percent of the plant's business, were once its
major product. Today the county facility is the
world's largest manufacturer of easy-open
aluminum lids for beverage cans; the plant
turns out more than thirty-five million of them
a day. Photo by Scott Mason; courtesy of the
Winchester Star

Royal Crown Cola Bottling Works of Winchester opened in 1928 on U.S. 11 north of Winchester and moved to its current site at Shawnee Drive in 1968. Its founder was William E. Bridgeforth, Sr. The company has remained in his family and today sells more than 2.5 half million 24-can cases of RC Cola, Dr. Pepper and Mountain Dew a year. It is the only non-Pepsi franchise that also bottles Mountain Dew.

Charles Haines, who worked at the plant for fifteen years, was eighty-three when this photo-graph appeared in the Winchester Star in 1982. He had retired from his job for two days, did not like retirement, and went back to work. He has since retired permanently. Haines was born on Potato Hill (now South Cameron Street) in 1899 and worked at the Virginia Woolen Mill for twenty-three years. He took a job at Royal Crown when the mill closed. Photo by Jessica Sullivan; courtesy of the Winchester Star

The Garber Ice Cream Company opened at North Cameron and Piccadilly streets in 1934 and later moved to its current site on U.S. 522 south of Winchester. Its founder, Charles E. Garber, was born in 1884. He was a Shawnee District representative to the Frederick County Board of Supervisors. His family continued to operate the business after he died in 1969. Pictured here are his sons, Donald E. Garber (eating an ice cream sandwich), who is president of the company; and Julian F. Garber (wearing a hat), who died in 1985. The company produces ice cream sandwiches, ice cream cones, and thirty-five flavors of ice cream. It can churn out eight hundred gallons of ice cream an hour and sells about one million gallons a year. Donald Garber provided the photograph of his father. Photo of Julian Garber by Larry Sullivan; photo of Donald Garber by Rick Foster; courtesy of the Winchester Star

Stuart M. Perry (1892-1954) opened a rock quarry in 1936 west of Winchester on old U.S. 50 (now State Route 803). The business continues to be run by his family. It has about ninety employees and produces more than five hundred thousand tons of crushed limestone a year. Photo by Scott Mason; courtesy of the Winchester Star

Fairs & Rural Organizations

Lawson S. "Doc" Triplett, Sr., was twelve years old when he posed for this picture with Carter Hall Mascot, the Grand Champion of the 1913 Winchester Fair. The photograph was taken at John Cather's farm on Merriman's Lane, which is where former Seventh District Rep. J. Kenneth Robinson lives. Triplett, who worked for Cather for six dollars a month, took the bull to the fair, which then was held on North Loudoun Street, just north of the Winchester Cold Storage. "He walked him there and he led him back," said his son, William F. Triplett of Mountain Falls, who provided this photo.

The modern county fair is an annual celebration of rural life and agricultural achievement. Youngsters and adults alike look forward to the week of country music, calf scrambles, beauty contests, livestock shows and good, old-fashioned fun. In the months before the fair, the Frederick County Fair Association plans the event, and members of organizations such as the 4-H, the Future Farmers of America, and Extension Homemakers work on their entries.

Fairs in Frederick County are a tradition that dates back to colonial times. The General Assembly act that established Winchester as a town in 1752 specified that fairs be held twice a year to increase the town's trade and benefit its inhabitants. "All manner of cattle, victuals, provisions, goods, wares, and merchandizes" were to be sold. So no one would stay away, people who had debts or were wanted for crimes would be immune from "arrests, attachments and executions."

The first Frederick County Fair at the current fairgrounds on U.S. 11 at Clearbrook was held in 1972. It was preceded by the Winchester Fair that the Shenandoah Agricultural Society first held about 1871 on land west of North Loudoun Street and north of the Winchester Cold Storage between modern day Commercial Street and Morningside Drive. The Winchester fairgrounds, which had a large grandstand and a track for harness horse racing, were sold in May 1939.

Later fairs were co-sponsored by 4-H and FFA clubs and were held at various locations, including the Stephens City School. The first annual Frederick County Agricultural Fair was held in 1948 at the Winchester Armory and was held there every year until 1965. No fairs were held from 1966 to 1968, until the first Frederick County Youth Fair was held at the Farmers Livestock Exchange in 1969. It was held there through 1971. In 1972, the fair moved to nineteen acres, south of Stonewall School, that were owned by the Stonewall Ruritan Club. The Frederick County Fair Association bought twenty-two acres next to the Ruritan property and north of the Kenilworth estate in 1973.

Over the years a number of buildings have gone up at the two sites, beginning with the Ruritan building. The county 4-H and FFA clubs constructed two buildings in 1974, and two more buildings were added in 1975 with donations from the Lee Whitacre family and the Gainesboro Ruritan Club. The Poultry Building was constructed in 1979 primarily with funds from the R. E. Aylor FFA Chapter. In 1981, the Gainesboro Ruritan Club built a forty-foot addition to the cattle barn and the county 4-H and Homemakers clubs built a picnic shelter. The fair's office building was constructed in 1987.

More than 11,000 people attended the fair on July 29, 1987, the largest attendance for one day in its history. The largest weekly attendance was 44,799 in 1986.

Youthful onlookers surround disc jockey Roy Nester, sitting behind the sign, and engineer Phil Whitney, left, as they produced a live broadcast of WRFL-WINC radio circa 1960 from a makeshift studio during the Frederick County Fair, which was held at the Winchester Armory from 1948 to 1965. WINC was the first local radio station, opening in 1941. Courtesy of the Winchester-Frederick County Historical Society

The Frederick County Fair in 1987 as seen from the top of the ferris wheel. Photo by Wendy Gavin Gregg; courtesy of the Winchester Star

The Middle Road Extension Homemakers Club was fifty years old when this photograph of four longtime members was taken in 1978. The Middle Road club is one of the oldest homemakers groups in Frederick County. Pictured here are, left to right, Helen Rinker Snapp, Virginia Lowe, and Helen Richards, and, standing, Virginia Bauserman. The photograph was taken at Relief United Methodist Church, where the organization has met since its founding in 1938. Snapp, Bauserman, and Lowe are charter members of the club. Courtesy of Winifred Smith

Ruritans Ted Cox (left) and Ralph Frye are shown rebuilding chimneys in Cabins, West Virginia, following devastating floods in November 1985. Cox is a member of the Back Creek Ruritan Club and Frye is a member of the Round Hill Ruritan Club. The photo was taken by Warren Driver, a member of the Round Hill club who also helped with the rebuilding. Courtesy of Ralph Frye

Agnes V. Shirley was a Frederick County extension agent from 1946 until she retired in 1969. Born near Berkeley Springs, West Virginia, she helped hundreds of 4-H and Extension Homemaker club members with projects ranging from soil conservation to cooking and sewing. She received a teaching certificate from Shepherd State Teacher's College in Shepherdstown, West Virginia, and then received a bachelor's degree with a major in home economics and a minor in biology from West Virginia University in Morgantown. She put herself through college by teaching school in Morgan County and doing part-time 4-H work in Berkeley, Jefferson, and Morgan counties. Courtesy of the Frederick County Extension Office

The officers of the Round Hill Ruritan Club Ladies Auxiliary after they were installed in August 1972 at the Round Hill Community Center. This group is believed to be one of the first Ruritan ladies auxiliaries in the country. Pictured in this photograph, which ran in the Northern Virginia Daily, are, from left to right, club directors Nancy Porterfield, Viva Cather, and Margaret Douglas, treasurer Helen Lutz, secretary Mary Brumback, president Genevieve Larrick, and vice president Etta Davis. Courtesy of Ralph Frye

Members of the Gore Spirits 4-H Club made this sign and placed it on U.S. 50 west of Winchester in 1982. From left, with their ages at the time of the photograph are (front row) Aneta Hahn, eleven; Tracey Lineburg, ten; Tony Lepley, twelve; (back row) Dwain Hahn, sixteen; Scott Lewis, twelve; Corey Corbin, fifteen; and Leroy Spittler, thirteen. Photo by Ray K. Saunders; courtesy of the Winchester Star

Patsy Cline rode in the Shenandoah Apple Blossom Festival parade with the Melody Playboys, a local group that she performed with before her rise to fame. Their convertible is headed south on North Braddock Street. This photograph, taken circa 1955, is provided by courtesy of Mel Dick, Cline's brother-in-law.

Cline was born Virginia Patterson Hensley in Gore on September 8, 1932, and grew up on South Kent Street in Winchester. Her rise to stardom is legendary and her songs are still popular today. The "Patsy Cline's Greatest Hits" album had sold more than one million copies by 1988. In 1985, Home Box Office made *Sweet Dreams*, a film based on Cline's life that earned Jessica Lange an Academy Award nomination for best actress.

Cline got her start in country music by singing with local bands and in talent contests at the old Palace Theater in Winchester. The applause meter froze when she made her debut on the Arthur Godfrey show.

Before her death on March 5, 1963 in an airplane crash near Camden, Tennessee, she was named the top female country singer for 1962 and had sung at Carnegie Hall and on Dick Clark's "American Bandstand." She received six top awards at the National Country Music Festival in 1962, and her song "I Fall to Pieces," was the number one song of 1961. Among her other hits were "Crazy," "Sweet Dreams," and "Walking After Midnight."

After her father left home, Cline, at the age of sixteen, dropped out of Handley High School and worked at Gaunt's Drug Store to support her family. The name Cline came from her first husband, Gerald Cline, whom she divorced. In 1957, she married Charlie Dick, who was born in Whitehall and worked as a linotype operator at the *Winchester Evening Star*

A bell tower at Shenandoah Memorial Park stands as a testament to Patsy Cline. Fans, some of whom came from as far away as Canada, stood in the rain to watch the dedication ceremony on September 6, 1987. Cline is buried at a nearby grave where her legal name, Virginia Dick, appears on the tombstone and the name Patsy Cline is in parentheses. Until the tower was built, the only other local monument to Cline were the gates at the entrance of the cemetery, which were paid for by her family. Photo by Rich Cooley; courtesy of the Northern Virginia Daily

This stretch of U.S. 522 south of Winchester looks almost empty in this recent photograph. But when Patsy Cline was buried at Shenandoah Memorial Park on March 10, 1963, thousands of people lined both sides of the five-mile funeral route from downtown Winchester. There were still more cars south of the cemetery and along Paper Mill Road. "Patsy got a funeral worthy of royalty," concluded a story in the Winchester Evening Star.

In 1987 the Frederick County Board of Supervisors named seven miles of the highway between U.S. 50 and Double Toll Gate for Cline. The road was dedicated at the same time as the bell tower. In 1987 developers C. Douglas Adams and Al Kassabian also opened Patsy Cline Drive, a street between South Pleasant Valley Road and Apple Blossom Mall, and dedicated it in 1988. Photo by Teresa Lazazzera

Buck Ryan, a resident of Stephens City, was a three-time national fiddle champion in the 1950s and a performer on the Jimmy Dean country music show with Dean and the Texas Wildcats. Born Arnold W. Ryan in 1925 in Conicville, he grew up in Mt. Jackson and started playing the fiddle at the age of seven. By the time he was fourteen he already had a following in the Shenandoah Valley and had gotten his first radio break on WSVA in Harrisonburg. Ryan also performed on radio in North Carolina in the mid-1940s and at WINC in Winchester. His 1951 performance at the National Guard Armory in Washington, D.C., led to his association with Jimmy Dean and the Texas Wildcats. Ryan later performed on the ABC network. In 1981, Dean, most members of the original Wildcats band, and country star George Hamilton IV put on a benefit for Ryan in Winchester and sold out two shows. Ryan died in 1982. Courtesy of Dalton W. Brill

176

Realist painter John Chumley was born in 1928 in Rochester, Minnesota, grew up in Knoxville, Tennessee, and came to Frederick County in 1961. Rural scenes of the Shenandoah Valley were often the subject of his canvasses. He is shown here painting Paris, Virginia, from the top of the Blue Ridge Mountains.

Chumley lived at the Vaucluse estate south of Stephens City and died in 1984. His work includes tempera, watercolor, oil, and pastel paintings. He studied at the Pennsylvania Academy of Fine Arts in Philadelphia and the Ringling School of Art in Sarasota, Florida, and was the artist in-residence at the Fort Worth Art Center. He received national recognition at his first New York exhibition in 1962, including notice from a Time magazine art critic, who said Chumley had a "lyric brush." His paintings hang in museums, galleries, private collections, and U.S. embassies throughout the world. Courtesy of his wife, Bettye Chumley

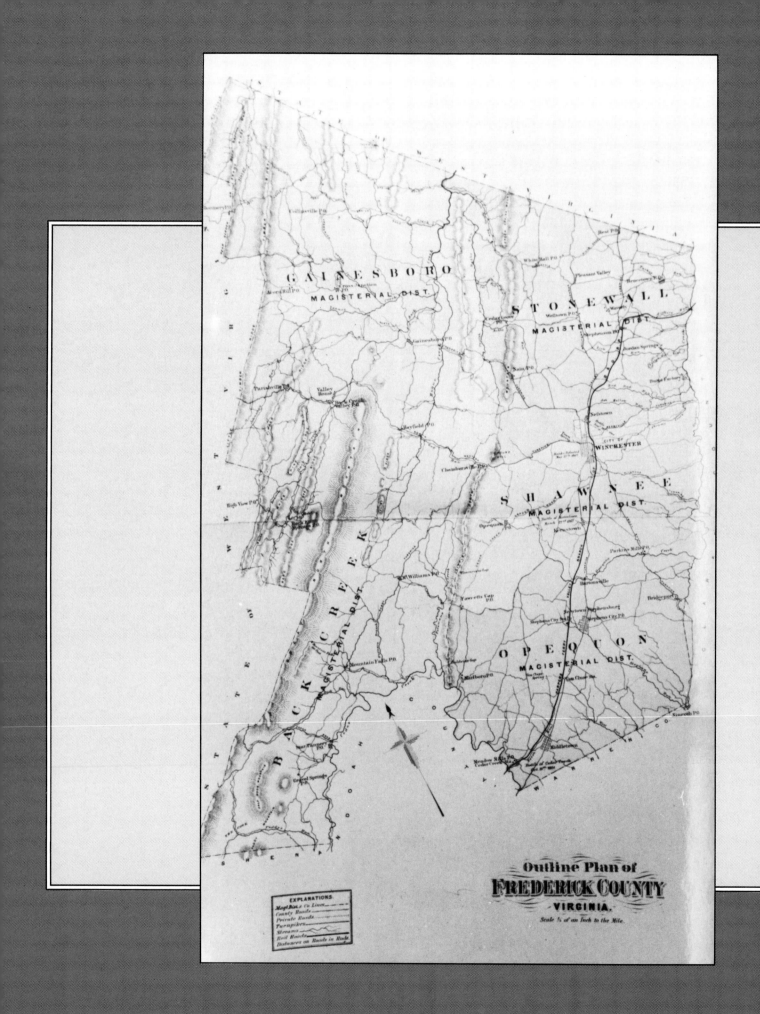

Outline Plan of
FREDERICK COUNTY
VIRGINIA.

Scale ½ of an Inch to the Mile.

s map shows Frederick County's five magis-
l districts as they appeared in Lake's Atlas
385.

On February 20, 1980, Winchester Mayor
Stewart Bell, Jr. (seated on left), and Frederick
County Board of Supervisors Chairman
S. Roger Koontz (seated on right) signed the
agreement that allowed the Frederick-
Winchester Judicial Center to be built.
Witnessing the signatures are, from left,
Winchester Councilman J. Thomas Kremer,
Jr., Supervisors R. Thomas Malcolm and
Kenneth Y. Stiles, and Councilman Roy W.
Bayliss, Jr. Besides sharing the cost of the
facility, the city agreed not to annex county
land for twenty years. The city also gave the
county an option to build offices in front of the
judicial center, and the county donated land
across from the judicial center where the city
built Court Square Autopark. Courtesy of
S. Roger Koontz.

On October 5, 1899, members of the Frederick County Board of Supervisors and the Winchester City Council put to rest the controversy over which locality owned the public square in downtown Winchester and signed an agreement that allowed Rouss City Hall to be built at the site of the old markethouse. The controversy arose more than a decade before, when the city removed the hitching yard between the Frederick County Courthouse and the old markethouse. The county received nine thousand dollars, a deed for all the public square except the land for City Hall, the right to hold circuit court and have a court clerk's office in City Hall, and an option on land at Cameron and Boscawen streets for a hitching yard. The city received thirty thousand dollars from Charles B. Rouss to build City Hall and the town clock. From left, front row: Clark Cather, W. P. Whitacre, William McCann, H. E. Boyd, R. E. Byrd, and William McGuire. Back row: William H. Dinges, A. R. Pendleton, R. M. Ward, T. K. Cartmell, T. E. Morrison, George H. Kinzel, James M. Haymaker, C. A. Heller, and James Cather. Courtesy of the Winchester-Frederick County Historical Society

Aerial view of the Frederick-Winchester Judicial Center (left foreground) and Rouss City Hall (across the street) with the Kurtz building on the left corner of the parking lot between them. Court Square Autopark is left of the judicial center. The old Frederick County Courthouse is behind City Hall. Photo by Larry Sullivan; courtesy of Photography by Cookie and Larry Sullivan

Virginia is changing quickly, and Frederick County is changing with it. People are moving to the state at the rate of five hundred people a day, according to a January 3, 1988, story in the *Richmond Times Dispatch*, giving Virginia one of the nation's most mobile populations. Those who are moving here are young, affluent, and well educated. Their backgrounds and outlooks are diverse, bringing changes in the state's ways of life, social attitudes, economy, culture, and politics.

One of the areas that is seeing the most dramatic growth, development, and change is Northern Virginia, and Frederick County is at its back door. It is only an hour from Dulles International Airport, whose business is expected to increase dramatically and where office complexes already are springing up in anticipation of the growth.

Throughout this century, farms in Frederick County have been turned into subdivisions, shopping centers, and industrial parks. The commercial and industrial strip from Valley Avenue to Kernstown and the business zone that has sprung up along Berryville Avenue bear little resemblance to the rolling countryside that lined those entrances to Winchester just half a century ago. What used to be fields at the eastern border of Winchester and Frederick County have become Delco Plaza, Apple Blossom Mall, Shenandoah College and Conservatory, and a cluster of roads and motels. In 1988, the Winchester-Frederick County Chamber of Commerce recommended that a convention center be built in that area.

Vacant commercial and industrial land along the south end of Pleasant Valley Road remain to be developed. There also are two industrial parks with nearly five

The Frederick-Winchester Judicial Center, bordered by Cameron, Boscawen and Kent streets, was dedicated on October 20, 1984. It is believed to be the first time that Virginia localities with separate courts jointly built a courthouse. The cost of the 81,000-square-foot building was $6.7 million. A study for a joint facility began in 1978 after Robert K. Woltz, chief judge of the Twenty-sixth Judicial Circuit, told the city and county that they had to provide better court facilities. Photo by Teresa Lazazzera

hundred acres of vacant land south and northeast of Winchester Regional Airport. Fort Collier Industrial Estates and Stonewall Industrial Park north of Winchester also are continuing to grow.

More houses are cropping up throughout Frederick County. The sections that have seen the most growth, and where most of the development is expected to continue, are eastern Frederick County, especially east of Stephens City, along Va. 7, and along Senseny Road between Stephenson and Sulphur Springs Road. Residential development is expected to follow Winchester Medical Center when it relocates to Amherst Street in 1989. Plans have been drawn for more than one thousand homes, townhouses, and condominiums on the west side of Winchester. Apartment and townhouse developments are being built on the southern end of the city.

The construction of new highways aided the area's growth. Interstate 81 was built in 1962-1968, replacing U.S. 11 as the area's main highway and following the path of a centuries-old road that linked the Shenandoah Valley to points north and west. Interstate 66, which was completed in the early 1980s, stops at Middletown, linking southern Frederick County to Northern Virginia and Washington, D.C. Va. 37, a western bypass around Winchester, was built in sections between 1967 and 1977. Officials are now talking about extending the route east. U.S. 522 north of Winchester is being widened to four lanes from Cross Junction to the West Virginia line.

Frederick County Sheriff William J. Newcome was shot to death the night of February 12, 1938, less than a year after taking office, while trying to arrest a man in Mountain Falls. He died almost instantly and never had a chance to draw his revolver.

Newcome was born in 1891 in Opequon District. He had been a deputy sheriff for four years when he was appointed sheriff on March 18, 1937, replacing Harry McCann, who became county treasurer. He died while trying to serve a warrant on George Pingley, who had been charged with selling sheep on which another man had made a levy.

Pingley was arrested the next morning for killing Newcome and critically wounding a state policeman. He was taken to an undisclosed jail south of Winchester after a crowd gathered at the police station. Courtesy of the Winchester-Frederick County Historical Society

Robert L. DeHaven was a law enforcement officer for thirty-five years, including twenty as sheriff of Frederick County and nine years as a deputy sheriff. He was born in 1902 in Gainesboro and died in 1974. He was a deputy to Sheriff John B. Bywaters from 1938 until the sheriff's death in 1947, when he was appointed to fill Bywaters' unexpired term. DeHaven was elected in November of that year, reelected in succeeding elections, and remained as sheriff until his retirement in 1967. Courtesy of the Handley Library Archives

Separate Places in an Era of Regional Cooperation

Frederick County and Winchester almost became one place in 1969. On September 9 of that year, members of the Frederick County Board of Supervisors and the Winchester City Council almost unanimously agreed that the two localities should merge and called for a special election.

County voters soundly defeated consolidation in a referendum on December 9, 1969. The county, however, lost a 1970 annexation court battle with the city, which took about five square miles of the county at its borders on January 1, 1971. About forty-five hundred people became city residents.

Future annexations were delayed through the year 2000 when city and county officials signed an agreement on February 20, 1980, to build the Frederick-Winchester Judicial Center. It is believed to be the first time that two jurisdictions in Virginia with separate courts have joined to build a common courthouse. As part of the agreement, the county also was given an option to build future offices on Cameron Street in front of the Judicial Center. In return, the city promised to make up for parking that had been lost when the center was built and constructed the Court Square Autopark on land that it received from Frederick County.

At the time, Winchester Mayor Stewart Bell, Jr., said the judicial center agreement was significant because it showed that the city and county could deal with common problems without sacrificing their identities.

"To me, the joint court facility we intend to build will stand as a visible witness to the real unity and common interest which underlie and must shape the relationship of Winchester and Frederick County," Bell said. "We are, in a thousand ways, one community. We live here side by side. We move from one jurisdiction to the other without discrimination. Our citizens do business day by day with one another. Our lives are enriched because of our common undertakings and many mutual relationships. Neither the city nor the county can prosper if the other languishes. As the years come and go we suffer under the same calamities, we prosper under the same benign influences."

While the city and the county did not merge, the two jurisdictions have joined together and with other neighboring localities to finance a number of regional projects. By sharing costs, they have been able to build larger facilities while reducing the financial hardships.

Besides the judicial center, other projects that were jointly sponsored by the city and county are the Winchester-Frederick County Visitor Center, which opened in 1987, and the Opequon Regional Wastewater Treatment Plant, which opened in 1988 and required millions of dollars in federal funds.

Among the projects that Winchester and Frederick County operate with Clarke County are the landfill and the Handley Library. They are also working on a regional jail. Representatives of Winchester and Frederick, Clarke, Warren, and Shenandoah counties make up the Winchester Regional Airport Authority and fund the airport's capital improvements.

Roscoe L. Bruce was elected sheriff of Frederick County in 1979 and was reelected to a second term in 1983 before being defeated by a wide margin in 1987. A Democrat, he won more than 50 percent of the vote in his first two elections, including his 1983 race against two opponents.

Born in 1928, Bruce is a native of Page County and an Army veteran. He was a state trooper for twenty-nine years before becoming sheriff. He was named Officer of the Year by the Winchester Exchange Club in 1982 and was cited for reorganizing the Sheriff's Department and adding services such as scuba diving and emergency response teams. Courtesy of the Winchester Star

Charles L. Sturdivant got a victory lift from two supporters when he was elected sheriff in 1987. Carrying Sturdivant on their shoulders during a Republican victory celebration are Charles Smith (left) and Del Frye. A former deputy, Sturdivant received 73 percent of the ballots cast and unseated his ex-boss, incumbent Roscoe L. Bruce. Sturdivant was born in 1944 in Portsmouth, where his parents welded ships for the Navy. They moved to Fairfax when he was three and to a farm in Frederick County in 1960. Sturdivant was drafted in 1965 and saw combat in Vietnam, receiving the Vietnam Service Medal and Good Conduct Medal. Sturdivant later worked for the Front Royal Police Department, was put in charge of investigations, and was recognized in 1980 by the Front Royal Optimist Club for distinguished service. He joined the Frederick County Sheriff's Department in 1981, was promoted to shift sergeant, and resigned in 1987 to run for sheriff. Photo by Scott Mason; courtesy of the Winchester Star

Whitacres have controlled the Frederick County Circuit Court Clerk's office and have been local Democratic leaders for nearly half a century. Lee N. Whitacre retired as clerk in 1967 and his son, George (pictured above), a deputy clerk, was elected to replace him. He was reelected to eight-year terms in 1975 and 1983.

Whitacre was born in 1911 and is a graduate of Handley High School and Shepherd College. He taught school for several years before becoming a deputy clerk in 1952. He is an owner of Shawnee Cannery in Cross Junction. Courtesy of the Winchester Star

Charles Meredith "Charlie" Rosenberger was a Back Creek representative to the Frederick County Board of Supervisors for twenty-four years and its chairman for sixteen years. A Democrat, he was first elected in 1931. He retired at the age of eighty-three.

Rosenberger was born in 1876 at Homestead, his family home on State Route 600 in western Frederick County, and died in 1966. He built a general merchandise country store across from the house, and the post office of Rosenberger, Virginia was established there in 1887. He was postmaster from 1899 until the post office closed in 1915.

Rosenberger was a member of the Fremont Lutheran Church for sixty-eight years and a trustee for fifty years. He was elected to the Joint Church Council of the Gravel Springs Lutheran Charge and served for sixty-five years, many of them as chairman. He also was a member of the county School Board, the Board of Public Welfare, and the board at Winchester Memorial Hospital. Courtesy of his daughter, Lt. Col. (ret.) Fietta Rosenberger

Lee and Lula Braithwaite Whitacre posed for this photograph before Lee died in 1974. Whitacre, a Democrat, was clerk of the Frederick County Circuit Court from 1942 until he retired in 1967. He taught school for twelve years before becoming a deputy commissioner of revenue in 1921, was elected commissioner of revenue in 1929, and held that office until he was appointed court clerk in 1941. He was returned to office in succeeding elections.

Whitacre was born in 1881 in Whitacre, a western Frederick County community named for his ancestors. The couple were married on December 24, 1908, having driven from Cross Junction to Winchester through a foot of snow. They had five children. Lulu Whitacre was born in Cross Junction in 1885 and taught school for three years. In recent years she was the oldest delegate to the county Democratic Committee's nominating conventions. She cast her first ballot in 1920, the year women were first allowed to vote. More than two hundred people attended her one hundredth birthday party in 1985. She died on June 1, 1988. Courtesy of the Winchester Star

Demands Created by Growth

As Frederick County has grown, greater demands have been placed on county government to provide services. Its annual operating budget has grown from $1.7 million in the 1961-1962 fiscal year to $50 million in 1987-1988. Education is its largest expenditure.

Fire and rescue services have relied almost entirely on volunteers since the first county fire company was established in Stephens City in 1939. Today there are 270 volunteers and ten fire companies. One of them, Middletown, also has a rescue squad, which answers calls in southern Frederick County. The Winchester Volunteer Rescue Squad responds to calls in the city and the rest of the county. Emergency medical technicians also are based at each fire station, and a first-responder program, created to assist the rescue squads, consists of trained volunteers who administer first aid, cardiopulmonary resuscitation and other lifesaving techniques. They are especially important in remote rural areas, where help may take longer to arrive.

Winchester and Frederick County already have a central dispatch system for fire and emergency calls and a 911 emergency calling system. Chesapeake & Potomac Telephone Company is installing an enhanced 911 system that will give rescuers precise directions to county homes. There currently is no house numbering system for the county and rescuers are often delayed from reaching their destination because they do not have good directions.

Winchester, whose fire companies date to the nineteenth century, now uses both paid and volunteer firefighters. The salary of the fire chief and other paid firemen are part of the city budget. The Middletown Fire Company and Rescue Squad has two paid men who are both firefighters and rescuers. Their salaries are paid with funds raised by the company.

In 1987, Frederick County hired its first paid fire and rescue worker, Homer Sanders, as a part-time emergency services coordinator. Government and fire association officials predict that the county will soon go to a system that relies on both paid and volunteer firefighters and that salaries for paid firemen will be part of the county's budget. While they hope to continue attracting volunteers, paid firefighters are especially needed in the more populated areas of Frederick County.

While the county's population is growing, the volunteer fire and rescue squads have been hurt in recent years by a decline in the number of new volunteers. They are deterred by increased training that state and federal agencies require of fire and rescue personnel. Many people also work in Northern Virginia and neighboring

S. Roger Koontz was the first chairman of the Frederick County Board of Supervisors to be chosen by the voters. Prior to his election in 1975, chairmen were supervisors who were chosen by the other board members. He is shown presiding over a meeting in the late 1970s. Raymond L. Fish, a Republican and a former Gainesboro representative, is on his left.

Koontz was principal of Middletown Elementary School from 1960 to 1968, Stonewall Elementary from 1969 to 1974, and Apple Pie Ridge Elementary from its opening in 1974 to his retirement in 1983. He also taught history at James Wood High School from 1951 to 1958 and was coach for baseball, football, and debate teams.

Koontz was born in 1920 in Ellicott City, Maryland. He ran twice for the House of Delegates in the early 1970s, first as a Republican and then as an independent. He was elected to the board as a Democrat and served two terms as chairman from 1976 to 1984. Courtesy of the Winchester Star

communities, making it difficult for them to volunteer. Newcomers from urban areas with services paid by county or city governments also are unaccustomed to volunteer fire and rescue services.

The county's recreation services have grown in the last two decades but residents have not had a public swimming pool since the one at Clearbrook Park closed after the summer of 1978 because its soft gunnite bottom had cracked and deteriorated and the levee between the pool and the park's lake had worn away.

After nearly a decade of debate, the Board of Supervisors has set aside $1 million for pools to be built at both county parks and a fund drive for three hundred thousand dollars, called "Let's Pool Together," was launched in 1987 to pay the remaining cost.

The Parks and Recreation Department was formed in 1971 and the following year the county bought forty-three acres and leased another twelve acres on U.S. 11 for Clearbrook Park, its first public park. In 1974, 330 acres along State Route 277 east of Stephens City was purchased for a second park. It opened in 1977, was named Sherando Park in 1980, and was dedicated on May 16, 1981.

In 1987, the two parks received more than 150,000 visits. The number of people who use the parks is expected to rise in the coming years as the county and the parks grow.

Population

	Winchester	Frederick County	Combined
1745	***	***	4,000*
1800	***	***	24,744
1830	***	***	26,046
1840	***	***	14,242+
1850	3,857	12,118	15,975
1860	4,392	12,154	16,546
1870	4,477	12,019	16,496
1880	4,958	12,595	17,553
1890	5,196	12,684	17,880
1900	5,161	13,239	18,400
1910	5,864	12,787	18,651
1920	6,883	12,661	19,544
1930	10,855	13,167	24,022
1940	12,095	14,008	26,103
1950	13,841	17,537	31,378
1960	15,110	21,941	37,051
1970	19,429	24,107	43,536
1980	20,217	34,150	54,367
1986	20,200	36,900	57,100*
1990	21,600	40,800	62,400*
2000	22,600	46,000	68,600*
2010	21,800	53,000	74,800*

Sources:
1745 population: *A Separate Place: The Formation of Clarke County, Virginia*, by Warren R. Hofstra, p. 7; 1790–1986 population, U. S. Census Bureau; and 1990–2010, projections by the Virginia Department of Planning and Budget

  * Estimated
*** Separate figures unavailable
  + Clarke and Warren separated from Frederick County in 1836

Rhoda Whitacre Maddox was the first woman elected to the Frederick County Board of Supervisors. She was born in 1936 in Winchester. A Democrat, she served two terms as the Gainesboro District representative from 1980 to 1988.

Maddox has been a member of several advisory committees to state government, the U.S. Department of Agriculture, and the Extension Service. She is chairman of the board of the Virginia 4-H Foundation; the Volunteer Action Center of Winchester, Frederick and Clarke; and Ebenezer Christian Church.

She has received the Governor's Award for Volunteering Excellence, the National 4-H Alumni Award, the Virginia 4-H Alumni Award, and the Friend of Extension Award. Maddox was named woman of the year for 1986 by the Winchester Business and Professional Women. She has a bachelor's degree in mathematics from Lynchburg College and was a computer programmer from 1958 to 1965. Courtesy of the Winchester Star

Clearbrook dairy farmer Kenneth Y. Stiles was elected chairman of the Frederick County Board of Supervisors in 1983 and was reelected in 1987. He also is a member of the Planning Commission. He started the Frederick County Young Republicans Club in 1972 and was elected Stonewall District representative to the Board of Supervisors in 1977 and reelected in 1981. He ran unsuccessfully for the House of Delegates in 1979.

Stiles was born in 1944 in Sandy Hill, Maryland, and grew up on his grandfather's farm in Montgomery County before his father moved the family to Waverly Farm in 1967. Today he and his brothers operate the 375-acre dairy farm on State Route 672. He has a bachelor's degree in dairy science from the University of Maryland, with minors in government and history. Courtesy of the Northern Virginia Daily

The Frederick County Board of Supervisors and other county officials in 1988. Front row, left to right, are County Administrator John R. Riley, Jr.; Back Creek District Supervisor Robert M. Rhodes, elected in 1983 and reelected in 1987; board Chairman Kenneth Y. Stiles, first elected to the board representing Stonewall District in 1977 and elected chairman in 1983 and reelected in 1987; and Stonewall District Supervisor Charles W. Orndoff, Sr., appointed to the board in early 1988. In the back row, left to right, are Commonwealth's Attorney and County Attorney Lawrence R. Ambrogi, who was appointed prosecutor in 1969 and won elections in 1971, 1975, 1979, 1983, and 1987; Gainesboro District Supervisor Roger L. Crosen, elected in 1987; Opequon District Supervisor Dudley R. Rinker, elected in 1987; Shawnee District Supervisor L. A. "Steve" Putnam, appointed to the board in early 1988; and Assistant County Administrator Stephen F. Owen. Ambrogi and all the supervisors are Republicans. Photo by Alan Lehman; courtesy of the Northern Virginia Daily

Secretary of the Army John O. Marsh, Jr., was born in Winchester in 1926 and grew up in Harrisonburg. He enlisted in the army in 1944 and served in the U.S. Occupation Forces in Germany after World War II. Marsh received a law degree from Washington and Lee University and practiced law in Strasburg and Richmond. Originally a Democrat, he was congressman of Virginia's Seventh District from 1963 to 1971 and a member of the House Appropriations Committee. He did not seek reelection and briefly returned to his law practice before receiving appointments from three Republican presidents. He became Richard Nixon's assistant secretary of defense for legislative affairs in 1973, Vice-President Gerald Ford's assistant for national security affairs in 1974, and President Ford's counselor with a cabinet rank in 1974 to 1977. Reagan appointed Marsh secretary of the army in 1981. *Courtesy of the Winchester Star*

Frederick County native and orchardist J. Kenneth Robinson represented the Seventh District in Congress from 1971 until his retirement in January 1985. A Republican, he was appointed in 1965 to the Virginia Senate seat vacated by Harry F. Byrd, Jr. He first ran for the congressional seat when Democratic veteran Burr P. Harrison retired in 1962 and was narrowly defeated by John O. Marsh, Jr.

Robinson was born in 1916, has a bachelor's degree from Virginia Tech, and is a World War II Army veteran. He was a state senator from 1965 to 1970. In the House of Representatives he was on the Appropriations Committee and was the ranking member of the Permanent Select Committee on Intelligence when he stepped down. In 1987 to 1988, he was honorary chairman of the Frederick County 250th Anniversary Commission. *Courtesy of the Winchester Star*

Harry F. Byrd, Jr., is the first person in the history of the U.S. Senate to be twice elected as an independent. In 1976 he received the largest vote ever given a Virginia candidate for any public office. A former Democrat, he left his party in 1970 rather than take an oath to support all party nominees.

Born in 1914 in Winchester, Byrd was the namesake of his famous father, a former governor and U.S. senator. He was a U.S. senator from 1965 to 1982 and a member of the Virginia Senate from 1948 to 1965. He entered Virginia Military Institute at sixteen and later attended the University of Virginia. During World War II, he was a Navy lieutenant

commander and executive officer of a patrol bombing squadron in the Central and Western Pacific.

Byrd was a state senator when he was appointed to his father's U.S. Senate seat. He was elected in 1966 as a Democrat and reelected in 1970 and 1976 as an independent. He was a member of the Senate Armed Services and Finance committees and the Joint House-Senate Committee on Taxation. Today he is chairman of the board of the Winchester Evening Star, Inc., and president and director of Rockingham Publishing Company. The business school at Shenandoah College and Conservatory is named for him. *Courtesy of the Winchester Star*

Henry Hudson Whiting of Winchester became the eighty-ninth justice of the Virginia Supreme Court on April 30, 1987. His son Brian, left, holds the Bible while Robert K. Woltz, chief judge of the Twenty-sixth Judicial Circuit, administers the oath of office at the Frederick-Winchester Judicial Center. He was the first person from Winchester appointed to the state's highest court in more than a century. The last was Thomas T. Fauntleroy in 1883. Born in Colorado in 1923, Whiting is a godson of

World War II Army Gen. George S. Patton, Jr., a descendant of early Virginia settlers, and a direct descendant of Henry Hudson, a seventeenth-century English explorer. He was in the army in Europe during World War II and is a graduate of the University of Virginia Law School. He practiced law in Winchester for thirty-one years before becoming a judge. Photo by Scott Mason; courtesy of the Winchester Star

Alson H. Smith, Jr., has represented Frederick County and Winchester in the House of Delegates since 1974. The chairman of the House Democratic Caucus, he has been ranked by newspaper polls as one of the most effective legislators in Virginia. He is a principal fundraiser for Democratic candidates.

Born in 1928 in Frederick County, Smith rose from humble beginnings to become a millionaire businessman. His father died when he was seven and Smith lived at his grandfather's home off Apple Pie Ridge with his mother and sister and three other families. A graduate of Handley High School, today he is chairman of the board of Shenandoah Foods, the franchisor of more than fifty Tastee Freez restaurants.

Smith is the sponsor of the bill designed to boost tourism by keeping schools closed until after Labor Day and a bill that saved Virginia millions of dollars by standardizing the design and construction of state facilities. He is chairman of the House Mining and Mineral Resources Committee and a member of the Appropriations Committee and chairman of its Capital Outlay Subcommittee. Photo by Richard Cooley; courtesy of the Northern Virginia Daily

Clearbrook Park began as a recreation facility for the employees of the Clearbrook Woolen Mill and became Frederick County's first public park. The county bought forty-three acres for the park, leased an adjoining twelve acres from Frey's Quarry, and opened the park the week of May 20, 1972. Officials marked the occasion with a spin around the lake. Leading the paddle boat procession are Supervisors Dennis T. Cole, left, and Richard Madigan. In the second boat,

left, is Wendell Dick, a member of the Frederick County Parks and Recreation Commission and later principal of James Wood High School-Amherst Campus, and County Administrator J. O. Renalds. In the back boat are Supervisor J. Robert Russell, left, and board Chairman Raymond C. Sandy. Photo by David B. Grim of the Winchester Star; courtesy of J. Robert and Colleen Russell

The first fire company in Frederick County was organized in 1939 in Stephens City and was chartered as the Independent Hose Company in 1941. Its first president was Robert E. Aylor, who also was the county superintendent of schools, and G. W. Lemley was the secretary. The name was changed to the Stephens City Fire Company in 1941. The company's first truck was a secondhand 1933 Dodge. The company now owns four modern vehicles, including the 1982 Pierce Arrow that is shown here. Courtesy of Margaret L. Weller

Frederick County Fire Companies and Rescue Squads

	Formed
Stephens City	1939
Middletown (fire company)	1941
Clearbrook	1947
Gore	1951
Middletown (rescue squad)	1952
Round Hill	1953
Winchester Rescue Squad	1957
Gainesboro	1958
Greenwood	1970
Star Tannery	1971
North Mountain	1973
Reynolds Store	1979

Frederick County made national headlines when a mountain of nine million tires off State Route 608 were set afire on the early morning of October 31, 1983. The tires erupted into this mushroom cloud, three hundred feet wide and forty-five hundred feet high, which could be seen as far away as Front Royal and Paris Mountain. The tires had been the topic of a decade-long debate between property owner Paul Rhinehart and county officials, who agreed earlier that year that Rhinehart could dispose of the tires in a smelting furnace provided that he accept no more tires after September 1. Known locally as the "Tarr Farr," it took from Halloween to the Fourth of July for the fire to burn itself out. The initial clean up cost was $1.7 million in federal money and $10,000 in county money. In 1987, Melvin Russell Jenkins of Frederick County pleaded guilty to setting the tire fire, to murder and to two other arsons. His total sentence was 110 years in prison, with 70 years to serve, 10 of them for the tire fire. In 1988, the Environmental Protection Agency recommended spending an additional $1.25 million to clean the site. Photo by Scott Mason; courtesy of the Winchester Star

James Wood High School Choir Director Paul S. Thompson directs the Concert Choir in front of the First Baptist Church during Preservation of Historic Winchester's Holiday House Tour in December 1987. Photos by Rick Foster; courtesy of the Winchester Star

Winchester's first nonalcoholic, family-oriented community New Year's Eve celebration was held December 31, 1987. More than two thousand people turned out for musical and dramatic entertainment held at various spots throughout Old Town Winchester and brought in the New Year with a midnight fireworks display. Gearing up for the fun are, from left, Frederick County Board of Supervisors Chairman Kenneth Y. Stiles, Winchester Mayor Charles M. Zuckerman, and organizer Kathy Nerangis. A Stephens City resident, Nerangis and her husband, Nick, own area McDonald's restaurants. She got the idea for the Winchester celebration after receiving a letter asking her to contribute to First Night Leesburg. Photo by Scott Mason; courtesy of the Winchester Star

Margaretta Carter Gaither (left) and Anna Bertha Cook Gravely are seen here during a May 22, 1988 reunion at Old Stone Presbyterian Church. They attended classes in the building on East Piccadilly Street when it housed Douglas School, Winchester's first black public school. Gaither was in the class of 1922 and Gravely was in the class of 1919. Both live in Winchester. The reunion was part of the church's two hundredth anniversary celebration. Built in 1788 and used today mostly for weddings and Christmas services, Old Stone began as an offshoot of Opequon Presbyterian Church, Frederick County's first church, and is now owned by First Presbyterian Church on South Loudoun Street, the congregation that evolved from Old Stone. Over the years it was a stable during the Civil War, the home of three Baptist churches, the first public school for blacks in Winchester and a drilling place for the Virginia National Guard. The Winchester Public School Trustees leased the church in 1875 and used the building as a public school for black children for more than fifty years. First called Free School or Old Stone College, the school housed grades one through nine and later was named Douglas School for black abolitionist Frederick Douglass. It was the predecessor of Douglas School on North Kent Street, a former all black school that was built in 1927 and remained segregated until 1966. The misspelled name was corrected when the facility became Frederick Douglass Elementary School in 1974. Photo by Wendy Gavin Gregg; courtesy of the Winchester Star

Members of Rosedale Baptist Church held Easter sunrise service on April 19, 1987, off U.S. 522 north of Winchester in Frederick County. The three crosses, twelve feet tall, are made of locust trees. They were fashioned by church member and county resident Lynn Durbin, an employee of Henkel-Harris Company. At the time, he said the crosses would remain on the land, which overlooks a pond and is owned by Paul and Lillian Wolfe. Photo by Rick Foster; courtesy of the Winchester Star

Winchester-area Catholics have attended mass at the Sacred Heart of Jesus Catholic Church since the basement was finished in 1870. The church, pictured left, is at Loudoun and Cecil streets and was dedicated on July 28, 1878. Fairs were held to raise money for it. The structure will be replaced in 1989 by a new church next to Sacred Heart Academy on Amherst Street but will still be used for weddings and occasional services. It was preceded by a stone church on National Avenue, built in 1805 behind the Old Stone Presbyterian Church on East Piccadilly Street. The first Catholic church was used as a stable by Union soldiers during the Civil War and was destroyed. Beginning as a mission of the Catholic Church at Harpers Ferry, West Virginia, Winchester's Catholic congregation grew as Irish workers arrived to build nineteenth-century turnpikes. Photo by Teresa Lazazzera

Kemesis of the Theotokos, the Virgin Mary Greek Orthodox Church, was organized in 1957. The congregation began with twenty-five families and first met at the Oddfellows Hall at Cameron and Boscawen streets. Services have been held at the current church, on Amherst Street, since it was finished in 1964. Members say it is the only Greek Orthodox Church in the United States that has no paid personnel. The congregation now has about fifty families and draws people from as far away as Front Royal, Martinsburg, West Virginia, and Hagerstown, Maryland. Photo by Teresa Lazazzera

The interior of the Beth El Temple (pictured on right) on Fairmont Avenue, the home of Winchester's Jewish congregation. The temple was dedicated in 1955. Before then, the congregation met at the Oddfellows Hall. Today the congregation consists of more than fifty families. Dan Isaac became its first full-time rabbi at Yom Kippur in 1987. Jews have been residents of Winchester since before the Civil War. Courtesy of Irv Lavitz

Aerial view of Winchester looking east, with Winchester Medical Center on Stewart Street in the foreground. Photo by Rudy Rodgers of Birds-Eye View

Frederick County and Winchester were named certified business locations in 1986 by the Virginia Department of Economic Development and signs, including this one, were placed at entrances to Winchester on U.S. 11, U.S. 50, Va. 7, and Winchester Regional Airport. The two localities were the fifth community in Virginia named to the program, which matches up businesses interested in moving to Virginia with communities that are able to meet their needs. Richard G. Dick (right), chairman of the Winchester-Frederick County Economic Development Commission, and Executive Director George Romine helped the city and county meet requirements for the designation, such as producing a marketing book and community maps. Photo by Scott Mason; courtesy of the Winchester Star

Loudoun Street at different seasons, different eras, and different angles. The modern photograph, looking south, shows shoppers undaunted by snow. The older photograph is looking north with the Farmers & Merchant's Bank on the right. It was taken circa 1910 during a Confederate Memorial Day celebration on June 6, an event that drew the largest crowds to town before the Shenandoah Apple Blossom Festival.

The center of Old Town Winchester has changed dramatically in the last 250 years. Beginning as a dirt road, it became Main Street and later a pedestrian mall. It has been hit hard in recent years by competition from shopping centers and shopping malls. In 1964, the City Council formed the Winchester Parking Authority to create more downtown parking and the Downtown Development Board to promote events, supervise improvements, and offer assistance to merchants. The Loudoun Street Mall was built in 1974 for five hundred thousand dollars. Business dropped in 1982 when downtown's largest stores, Leggett, Sears and J. C. Penney, left for the Apple Blossom Mall. Downtown Winchester has since rebounded by promoting itself as a district of specialty shops and independent merchants who offer personalized service. In 1985 Winchester was selected as one of five Virginia cities to participate in the state's new Main Street Program, which is aimed at downtown revitalization. It entitled the city to three years of free advisory assistance from the Virginia Department of Housing and Community Development and the National Main Street Center, an affiliate of the National Trust for Historic Preservation. Modern photo by Rick Foster; courtesy of the Winchester Star; older photo courtesy of Louise Stover Brim

Aerial view of Apple Blossom Mall, sur-
rounded by Interstate 81, South Pleasant
Valley Road, Patsy Cline Drive, and undeveloped commercially zoned land. Photo by
Rudy Rodgers of Birds-Eye View

George W. Ferguson, the manager of Apple
Blossom Mall, stands at the mall's food
court. The mall employs about twelve
hundred people and had eighty-seven stores
in 1988. Winchester's retail sales have
soared since it opened in 1982. In 1987, it
generated $72,362,300 in taxable retail
sales, or about one out of every four retail
dollars spent in the city. It is a regional
shopping center attracting people from surrounding counties and eastern West Virginia. Photo by Scott Mason; courtesy of
the *Winchester Star*

Taxable Retail Sales

	Winchester	*Frederick County*
1967	$41.5 million	$20.5 million
1977	$132.9 million	$63.0 million
1987	$329.1 million	$195.4 million

196

Valley Avenue as it looks today facing north from its intersection with Cedar Creek Grade and Weems Lane, and as Valley Pike, a toll road with stops such as Hillman's Tollgate, in a 1910s photograph. The tollgate building is at the current site of Stinson Electronics. Standing by the toll sign is Isaac H. Moore. His adopted niece, Pearl Brindle Stone, is seated to his left. Moore supervised the construction of nearby Middle Road and provided some of the equipment to build it. Older photo courtesy of Grace and Merle Moore; modern photo by Rick Foster; courtesy of the Winchester Star

Aerial view of eastern Frederick County, including Va. 7, one of the areas where development is expected to occur, and how Va. 7 looked in 1901, when it was Berryville Pike. Aerial by Rudy Rodgers of Birds-Eye View; older photo courtesy of the Winchester-Frederick County Historical Society

The Millbank Farmhouse survived the Civil War because its owner, Daniel T. Wood, was loyal to the Union. It was spared again in 1986 after local residents and members of Preservation of Historic Winchester (PHW) objected to the Frederick-Winchester Service Authority's plans to tear it down and the Environment Protection Agency threatened to withdraw millions of dollars in federal funds for the Opequon Wastewater Treatment Plant project. PHW has since launched efforts to restore the house, bringing Winchester's strong preservationist movement to Frederick County.

The farm, including the house, was condemned in 1984 to make way for construction of the plant. Known earlier as Spout Spring, it was on property along Opequon Creek that Joseph Carter settled in 1743 and where his heirs operated a mill. Daniel Wood's father, Isaac, owned the farm by 1836 and operated the mill there along with others on nearby Red Bud Run. Isaac and Daniel are believed to have built the brick house that is there today and may have incorporated parts of an earlier house built by Carter. Daniel Wood named the house Millbank. An April 10, 1863, order signed by Union Major Gen. Robert H. Milroy kept it from being destroyed in the Civil War. Photo by Rich Cooley; courtesy of the Northern Virginia Daily

The $31 million Opequon Regional Waste-water Treatment plant on Va. 7 opened in 1988. The Millbank House (on right) is west of the plant. Winchester operates the plant, which serves city residents and county residents east of the city and customers in Kernstown, including industries as far south as the General Electric plant. The sewage treatment facility was processing an estimated 4.1 million gallons of sewage a day when it opened, and Winchester officials predict the plant's treatment capacity of five million gallons a day will be reached by the early 1990s. Photo by Rudy Rodgers of Birds-Eye View

A Winchester & Western train is shown rounding the tracks in western Frederick County in this photograph taken on January 11, 1988. The train is hauling two separators, the largest objects ever hauled on the W & W. They were headed for Frye's Quarry in Clearbrook after being removed from Unimin Corporation's sand quarry at Gore. This photo was taken from U.S. 50 west of Round Hill. Photo by Scott Mason; courtesy of the Winchester Star

199

Pa Frederick and Ma Winchester, caricatures by L. Neill Woods, graced the pages of the Winchester Evening Star *during the second quarter of the twentieth century. Ma and Pa personified the characteristics of the small city and the rural county they were named for and illustrated the events, issues, and messages of the times. Pa Frederick courtesy of William Woods; Ma Winchester courtesy of the Winchester-Frederick County Historical Society*

Bibliography

BOOKS

Anderson, Rual. *Genealogy: Spaid, Anderson, Whitacre and a Number of Allied Families, Also Historical Facts and Memoirs*, by the Author, 1975.

Ansel, William H. Jr. *Frontier Forts Along the Potomac and its Tributaries*. Parsons, W. Va.: McClain Printing Co., 1984.

Carr, Clay Bryan, ed. *A Time to Remember 1927-1946*. Stephens City: Commercial Press, 1987.

Cartmell, T. K. *Shenandoah Valley Pioneers and Their Descendants, A History of Frederick County, Virginia from its Formation in 1738 to 1908*. Berryville, Va.: Chesapeake Book Company, 1963.

Chandlee, Edward E. *Six Quaker Clockmakers*. Philadelphia: The Historical Society of Pennsylvania, 1943.

Cohen, Stan *Historic Springs of the Virginias: A Pictorial History*. Charleston, W. Va.: Pictorial Histories Publishing Company, 1981.

Cohn, Capt. Douglas A. *Jackson's Valley Campaign*, Washington, D. C.: American Publishing Co., 1976.

Current, Richard N.; Williams, Harry T.; Freidel, Frank; and Brinkley, Alan. *American History, A Survey*, 2 vols., 6th ed. New York: Alfred A. Knopf, 1983.

Dabney, Virginius. *Virginia The New Dominion*. Garden City, N. Y.: Doubleday & Company, 1971.

Davis, Julia. *The Shenandoah*. Copyright 1945. Written for the Rivers of America series. Originally published by Farrar and Rinehart.

Durant, John and Alice. *The Presidents of the United States*, 2 vols. New York: A. S. Barnes and Co., Inc., 1955. Miami, Fla.: A. A. Gache & Sons, 1975.

Freeman, Douglas Southall. *Lee's Lieutenants*, New York: Charles Scribner's Sons, 1944.

Frost, Lawrence A. *The Phil Sheridan Album, A Pictorial Biolography of Phillip Henry Sheridan*. Seattle: Superior Publishing Co., 1968.

Gallagher, Gary W. *Stephen Dodson Ramseur Lee's Gallant General*. Chapel Hill, N. C.: University of North Carolina Press, 1985.

Gardner, William M. *Lost Arrowheads and Broken Pottery, Traces of Indians in the Shenandoah Valley*. Manassas, Va.: Tru Tone Publication, 1986. (A Thunderbird Museum Publication)

Gore, James Howard. *My Mother's Story: Despise Not the Day of Small Things*. Philadelphia: The Jedson Press, 1923.

Greene, Katherine Glass. *Winchester, Virginia and its Beginnings, 1743-1814* Sesquicentennial ed. Strasburg, Va.: Shenandoah Publishing House, 1926.

Hale, Laura Virginia. *The Revolutionary Years 1776-1781 in Old Frederick County, Virginia*. Copyright 1978 by Laura Virginia Hale. First appeared as articles in the Winchester Star for 1976 bicentennial celebration.

Hening, William Waller, ed., *A Collection of All the Laws of Virginia*, vol. 7. By the Editor, 1820.

Higginbotham, Don. *Daniel Morgan Revolutionary Rifleman*. Chapel Hill, N. C.: University of North Carolina Press, 1961.

Hofstra, Warren R. *A Separate Place. The Formation of Clarke County, Virginia*, Clarke County Sesquicentennial ed. Published by the Clarke County Sesquicentennial Committee, White Post, Va., 1986.

Hutton, James V. Jr. *Frederick County, Virginia, 1738-1988, Tell Me of a Land that's Fair*. Athens, Ga.: Iberian Publishing Co., 1987.

Hutton, James. V. Jr. *In the Shade of the Apple Tree*. Stephens City: Commercial Press, 1976.

Johnston, Wilbur S. *Milburn Methodist Chapel in Frederick County, Virginia*. Stephens City: Commercial Press, 1984.

Kercheval, Samuel. *A History of the Valley of Virginia*, 4th ed. Strasburg, Va.: Shenandoah Publishing House, 1925.

Kidney, Walter C. *Winchester: Limestone, Sycamores & Architecture*. Photography and Design by James R. Morrison. Winchester, Va.: Preservation of Historic Winchester, 1977.

Lacina, Thomas M., and Thomas, William C. *A History of Sacred Heart Parish*. Boyce, Virginia: Carr Publishing Co., 1953.

Lederer, John. *The Discoveries of John Lederer in Three Marches from Virginia to the West of Carolina*. London, 1672. Printed by J. C. for Samuel Heyrick at Grays-Inne-Gate, in Holborn.

Long, E. B. *The Civil War Day by Day*. Garden City, N. Y.: Doubleday & Co., Inc., 1971.

Lothrop, J. M. and Dayton, A. W. *Atlas of Frederick County, Virginia from Actual Surveys*. D. J. Lake & Comp., 1885.

Magill, Mary Tucker. *Stores from Virginia History*, Lynchburg, Va.: J. P. Bell Co., 1897

Mason, James M. *Public Life and Diplomatic Correspondence of James M. Mason*. New York and Washington, D. C.: The Neale Publishing Co., 1906.

McDonald, Cornelia. *A Diary with Reminiscences of the War and Refugee Life in the Shenandoah Valley 1860-65* Annotated and supplemented by Hunter McDonald. Nashville, Tenn.: Cullum and Ghertner Co., 1934.

McDonald, William N. *A History of the Laurel Brigade*. Published by Kate S. McDonald, 1907.

Moore, Frank. *The Portrait Gallery of the War*, New York: D. Van Nostrand, 1865.

Morton, Frederic. *The Story of Winchester in Virginia, The Oldest Town in the Shenandoah Valley*. Strasburg, Va.: Shenandoah Publishing House, 1925.

Mullin, Larry A. *The Napoleon of Gotham: A Study of the Life of Charles Broadway Rouss*. Winchester, Va.: Farmers and Merchants National Bank, 1974.

Norris, J. E. *History of the Lower Shenandoah Valley Counties of Frederick, Berrkeley, Jefferson and Clarke*. Chicago: A. Warner & Co., 1890. Berryville, Va.: Virginia Book Company, 1972.

Pickeral, J. Julian and Fogg, Gordon. *An Economic and Social Survey of Frederick County.* Berryville, Va.: Virginia Book Company. University of Virginia Record Extension Series. A Laboratory Study in the School of Rural Economics, 1930.

Ploski, Harry, and Williams, James, eds. *The Negro Almanac: A Reference Work on the Afro American.* 4th ed. New York: John Wiley & Sons, 1983.

Quarles, Garland R. *George Washington and Winchester, Virginia, 1748-1758, A Decade of Preparation for Responsibilities to Come. Winchester-Frederick County Historical Society Papers,* vol. 8, 1974.

Quarles, Garland R. *The Churches of Winchester, Virginia: A Brief History of Those Established Prior to 1825.* Prepared for the Farmers & Merchants National Bank, Winchester, Va., 1960.

Quarles, Garland R. *Occupied Winchester 1861-65,* Winchester, Va.: Farmers & Merchants National Bank, 1976.

Quarles, Garland R. *Some Old Homes in Frederick County, Virginia.* Prepared for the Farmers & Merchants National Bank, Winchester, Va., 1971.

Quarles, Garland R. *The Schools of Winchester, Virginia.* Prepared for the Farmers & Merchants National Bank, Winchester, Va., 1964.

Quarles, Garland R. *The Streets of Winchester, Virginia: The Origin and Significance of their Names.* Prepared for The Farmers and Merchants National Bank, Winchester, Va.

Russell, William Greenway. *What I Know About Winchester, Recollections of William Greenway Russell, 1800-1891.* Edited by Garland R. Quarles and Lewis N. Barton. Reprinted from the Winchester News by the Winchester-Frederick County Historical Society. Staunton, Va.: McClure Publishing Co., 1953. Winchester, Va.: Winchester Printer, 1972.

Schildt, John W. *Hunter Holmes McGuire Doctor in Gray.* Chewsville, Md.: By the Author, 1986.

Steele, Inez Virginia. *Methodism and Early Days in Stephens City, Virginia, 1732-1905.* Stephens City: George F. Norton Publishing Company, 1906.

Triplett, Ralph L. *A History of the Upper Back Creek Valley, Frederick County, Virginia Historical Series, Vol 1.* Cullman, Ala.: The Gregath Company, 1983.

Wallace, Lee A., Jr. *A Guide to Virginia Military Organizations 1861-65.* Richmond, VA.: Virginia Civil War Commission, 1964.

Warner, E. J. *Generals in Blue,* Baton Rouge, La.: Louisiana State University Press, 1964.

Warner, E. J. *Generals in Gray,* Baton Rouge, La: Louisiana State University Press, 1959.

Wayland, John W. *Twenty-five Chapters on the Shenandoah Valley.* 2nd ed. Harrisonburg, Va.: C. J. Carrier Co., 1976.

Weddell, Alexander Wilbourne, ed. *Virginia Historical Portraiture, 1585-1830.* Richmond: William Byrd Press, 1930.

Wert, Jeffrey D. *From Winchester to Cedar Creek: The Shenandoah Campaign of 1864.* Carlisle, Pa.: South Mountain Press Inc. Publishers, 1987.

Wilkins, James Richard Sr. *The Impossible Task: A History of Shenandoah College and Conservatory and the Relocation to Winchester, Va. 1875-1985.* Harrisonburg, Va.: Good Printers, 1985.

Winchester-Frederick County Historical Society, *Images of the Past, A Photographic Review of Winchester and Frederick County, Virginia.* Photos selected and researched by Michael Foreman, Virginia L. Miller, Reed Nester and Charles Thorne. Winchester-Frederick County Historical Society, 1980.

Winchester-Frederick County Historical Society, *Men and Events of the Revolution in Frederick County, Virginia,* vol. 2, Bicentennial Issue of the Winchester-Frederick County Historical Society Papers, 1975.

Winnemore, Lawrence P. *The Winchester & Western Railroad,* 1976.

Younger, Edward, ed. *The Governors of Virginia.* Charlottesville, Va.: University Press of Virginia, 1982.

BOOKLETS, PAMPHLETS AND BROCHURES

Davis, Isabel Hammock. *Long Glances Back: A Little History of Middletown Agricultural High School,* Middletown, Frederick County, Virginia, 1909-1950. Stephens City: Commercial Press.

Gordon, C. Langdon. *A Sketch of the Historic Opequon Presbyterian Church,* Winchester, Va., 1984.

History of the Confederate Memorial Association of the South. New Orleans, 1904.

Places of Worship, Winchester and Frederick County, Virginia, 1987-88. 2nd ed. Edited by Clay B. Carr and Mildred L. Carr, 1987.

Whitehorne, Joseph. *Guided Tour of The Battle of Cedar Creek.* Strasburg, Va: The Wayside Museum of American History and Arts, 1987.

Winchester-Frederick County Historical Society. *Historic Winchester and the Shenandoah Valley of Virginia,* 1982.

Winchester-Frederick County Civil War Centennial Commission. *Civil War Battles in Winchester and Frederick County 1861-65,* Winchester, Va., 1960.

Winchester-Frederick County Civil War Centennial Commission. *Civil War Battles in Winchester and Frederick County 1861-65,* Winchester, Va., 1960.

PERIODICALS

Barton, R. T. "Gabriel Jones: The Lawyer," *The West Virginia Historical Magazine,* April 1902, pp. 19-30.

Hassler, William W. "Dr. Hunter Holmes McGuire, Surgeon to Stonewall Jackson, the Confederacy and the Nation," *Virginia Cavalcade.* Richmond: The Virginia State Library, 1982.

Ritter, Ben. "The Widow's Favorite, *Civil War Times Illustrated,* February 1979, pp. 36-39.

The Winchester Star, clippings from the newspaper's files.

The Winchester Star, Northern Virginia Daily, The Washington Post, The Virginia Gazette, Winchester Advertiser, The Winchester Gazette, and *The Virginia Centinel,* clippings in the Handley Library Archives.

PUBLIC DOCUMENTS

Hutton, Jr. James V. *Local History Bulletin.* Winchester, Va: Frederick County Public Schools, 1968.

Newlon, Jr., Howard: Pawlett, Nathaniel Mason, et al. *Backsights.* The Virginia Department of Highways and Transportation, 1985.

Frederick County Comprehensive Plan, background reports. Frederick County Department of Planning and Development, 1987.

Population Abstract of the United States, McLean, Va.: Andriot Associate, 1980.

U.S. Department of Commerce. Bureau of the Census. *Census of Population 1980.*

Stephens City Comprehensive Plan 1985.

Middletown Comprehensive Plan 1985.

Index

About the Authors

Rebecca A. Ebert is a lifelong Winchester native. Serving presently as the archives librarian at the Handley Library, Ebert has been active in the Frederick County 250th Anniversary Commission, the Shenandoah Valley Historic Institute, and Advisory Council for the Shenandoah Valley History Project, and the Winchester Business and Professional Women.

She is a graduate of Handley High School, Radford College, and the University of Maryland, where she earned a double master's degree in history and library science. She is the co-author of *Finding Your People in the Shenandoah Valley* and is continuing research in black history and women's history in the community.

Teresa Lazazzera is a Realtor with ERA Jim Barb Realty. She was a staff writer for the *Winchester Star* from 1985 to 1993. She was born in Winchester, Virginia, and grew up in Clearbrook. She is the daughter of Italian immigrants.

A graduate of James Wood High School, Lazazzera has a bachelor's degree from the University of Virginia with a double major in history and Italian, a master's degree in Italian from the University of California at Los Angeles and a master's in journalism from the University of Southern California.

Lazazzera was president and station manager of WTJU-FM, the University of Virginia's noncommercial radio station and has held jobs and internships at radio and television stations in Charlottesville and Southern California. Before joining the *Star*, she was a writer for newspapers published by Pasadena Media Inc. and a reporter for WINC-Radio in Winchester. She received a third place award for Lifestyle Writing from the Virginia Press Association in 1985. She is chairman of Tri-County Virginia Opportunities Industrialization Center and former chairman of the Child-Parent Center of Winchester.

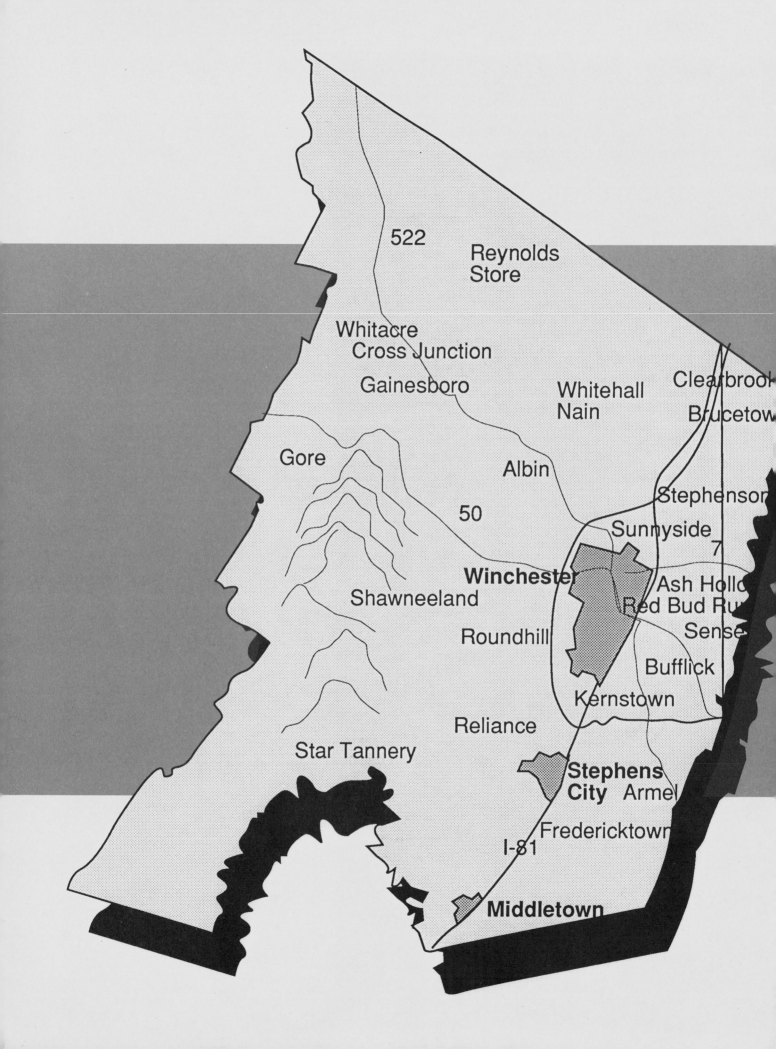